Establishing Your Frequency

By
Kelly C. Bowker

Kelly C. Bowker

DEDICATION

I dedicate this book to my team in non-physical. My guides and angels, for all of their love and kindness and patience as they brought me to the frequency that allowed me to receive these teachings. Especially Angel Ariel who held my hand as I melted down at the thought of bringing through the angel team. I now know you have been with me always…

Also by
K.C.Bowker
ReDefining Faith
Available on Amazon

CONTENTS

ACKNOWLEDGMENTS

I would like to thank all of my friends and family for their continued support. I would also like to thank all of the people in spirit who are looking for a voice. Thank you for finding me…

Establishing Your Frequency

Introduction

Well, it's November 2022 exactly one year since my therapist Maria encouraged me to look up what it meant to be an empath. That changed the course of my life forever! I've had a spiritual awakening. What does that mean? It means that I did enough personal work, I've healed enough of the wounds of childhood to clear the way for me to be able to hear my inner voice and develop a personal relationship with my team in spirit.

My first book told the story of my struggle to trust what was happening to me. Much of the book was direct transcriptions of downloads that I received from my guides during meditation. It told the journey from fear and doubt to confidence and clarity.

This is my second book! Until three months ago I had never written or published anything of any consequence! But one day back in August I got the impulse to sit down at my computer and start dictating. I wanted to tell my story; things had unfolded for me in such an extraordinary way that I couldn't imagine that my experiences wouldn't have a positive effect on other people who were perhaps going through a similar experience. At the very least I thought people might find it interesting!

I learned so much writing the first book. As I told my readers in that book, I have a daily relationship with my guides. Part of my morning routine is to spend time in meditation often channeling my guides and whatever message they might have for me that particular day. Sometimes it's run-of-the-mill information. How to live in the world, how to live closer to them. I often will ask questions and they will answer with their usual humor and insight. What that means is that I don't often go back and listen to the downloads once I have them. The process of writing the first book afforded me the opportunity to lay out the information in chronological order and to see how my guides and teachers were bringing me along to meet my goal. I wanted to be a medium. I had been experiencing nudges from a beautiful young woman in spirit named Cindy. I worked with her mother, and I knew that it would be very healing for her to have a reading and I wanted to be the one to do it. The first book is the story of how my guides and teachers gave me all the tools that I needed to succeed as a medium, and how I learned to trust the information that they gave me.

It was only yesterday that I received the e-mail confirming that my self-published book, ReDefining Faith, had been accepted and was available on Amazon for purchase. It left me feeling surreal... Truly in awe that this is now my life! I have no idea if the book will sell more than just a few copies to my friends and Facebook community, and I'm not terribly concerned to be honest. I feel like I had a calling to write my experiences down. I thought that had I had a book like this at the beginning of my journey it would have helped me a great deal.

The first book is finished so now what? I found myself staying busy throughout the day. I didn't do my meditation this morning. I was having fun receiving congratulatory comments and text messages from friends who saw my book posted on Facebook. My mind was going a hundred! There are so many different directions that I could take. I've thought about starting a YouTube channel, I've thought about doing a blog. What about advertising and promoting my book? Finally, I plopped my butt down in a chair and asked my guides what now?

Before I start there are several things I need to explain. First when I refer to my guides, I am talking about a collection of non-physical beings that I can communicate with. I am a channel, which means I can shift my consciousness and allow non-physical energy to speak through me. I refer to these transmissions as downloads. In my last book I was able to transcribe word for word what they were giving me. I am realizing something; I haven't transcribed any of my downloads since I finished Redefining Faith. As I am trying to transcribe now, I realize that my guides are communicating with me through a variety of methods now, only one of which is the spoken word. This threw me a bit! Initially I thought the second book would just pick up where the last book left off but that is not what they are telling me. They want us to create a book that gives some down-to-earth advice and direction on how to live in this world today. The format will be a bit different from the last book. I will take snippets and concepts from my downloads and then explain them. There are times when they give me big blocks of information that I can transcribe word for word. When the concepts and information become more complex, they have begun to drop blocks of information, I would call them knowings, into my mind. I realized when I tried to transcribe one of these downloads that it was very confusing as it came through. It wasn't confusing to me because I had the extra information they had placed in my mind that made me understand. When I transcribe something that is from my guides it will be italicized. When it is my words, it will be regular. If I break into a download with my own words, which I often do, I will put those words in parentheses and make the print regular. My non-physical team has their own way of speaking. I tried to "clean up" the things that made it really difficult to understand but I didn't want to take away their unique way of speaking. I apologize in advance if some of their downloads are hard to understand.

Chapter One

Where to Start

November 15, 2022

You are asking what your next step should be now that your first book is finished. We are very excited for you around this book because we know the satisfaction that it has given you in bringing it to fruition. (My jaw was trembling, that is one of the physical signs they give me when I channel) we celebrate you on your path. Knowing that you are following your heart's desire. Your heart's desire is to serve spirit. But you must remember dear one, that there is no need for spirit to be served. We are not saying that there is no value in bringing the message out into the world. We want to remind you that your purpose on this earth is for you to find your highest most joyful life. We want you to find joy Kelly. We did feel your joy as you published your book, and we know that there was great fun in that for you! There will be much success, we know that you question that even as we say it, but it will unfold in its way. There are not a lot of things for you to do to bring about that success. Just wait for the impulses, you are asking yourself if you need to be sifting through ideas for the various things that you can do on your spiritual path so that perhaps we can give you a ping on one and you will feel the inclination to go one direction or the other. There is nothing wrong with that Kelly. Just remember, moment by moment within your day we want you to feel the love that spirit has for you. We do not have a grand agenda. When you saw the unfolding of your book and it occurred to you that you were in training, that is because you had set an intention for yourself. Something that you wanted to be able to do and we were urging you along the path with the tools that you would need to accomplish that goal.

It all boils down to learning to follow your internal guidance. As humans we often question, should we go left or should we go right at any given time. Since I was a small girl, I felt the love in my heart for what I called God at that time, I knew I wanted to be spirit led. I wanted to navigate my life knowing that I had guidance and help from a higher being. I would pray and I would ask for help and advice and I would do my best to follow the right path.

What I have learned is that spirit always brings us back to the present moment. I'm not saying anything new when I say that humans have a compulsion to live in the past or the future. They are leading me to believe that they are going to give us some very concrete methods and strategies to live in the present moment and access higher guidance. They are truly putting me to the test, as I spend my time and energy working on this, not having any idea what it is going to contain! So dear reader we are in this together! But we have an incredible team of support that we are all able to access.

Let each day unfold, be in the moment. This morning when a negative thought crossed your mind, it reminded you to raise your energy. If you could learn a technique to maintain that higher level of energy throughout your day that would be the greatest gift that you could give to humanity. Spend some time thinking about that, how to live your life connected, how to raise your vibration and maintain it throughout your day, because you know how hard that is.

That is certainly true! I can get information directly from source energy and I still struggle to maintain my connection! I guess that is the human condition, to strive. We are all striving in one way or another. I hate negative thinking, but I fall into it just like everyone else. I hate those pretend arguments that go on in my mind when I tell someone off. I don't understand why so much of our time is spent with our brains running on a negative loop. I know if we could figure out how to stop that loop, we would certainly be better off.

So, I tried to do what they said around using the negative thought as a reminder to then reset my energy to a higher frequency and it helped throughout the day. I probably only remembered to do it five or six times throughout the entire day, but I guess that's better than nothing.

Set your intention for your highest good Kelly. Trust that we know your heart and we are supporting you and loving you on this journey. Trust that we hear your desires to hear and to see and to experience these extraordinary things. You have experienced many extraordinary things up to this point, have you not? You can start writing your next book. There is going to be value as you have already sensed in transcribing the downloads and spending time with the words on the page. It is part of your evolution Kelly, don't be obsessive about it. Remember the rule. The rule for your life, if it feels fun and exciting and you're having a good time doing it, then do it! It can take you years and that's fine. Don't let the human ego get involved, wanting things to be so much quicker because it shows something to the world...

Intention is very powerful! I have certainly been convinced of that over the last year. They have told me many times that a human's intention is one of their most powerful tools. So that's a good place for us to start. To set our intention, to follow these instructions as well as we can. I love that they always bring me back to joy, and fun. This is more than them wanting me to be happy. This is a very important part of the creative process. To follow your passion, your excitement and joy. When you are feeling those things, you can absolutely know that you are connected to source energy. When you consciously acknowledge that, it starts to create a connection between you and source energy. They are showing me tiny glistening threads of energy between the human and the cosmos. Each intentional thought has power, and it stays there. Meaning that over our lifetime with practice we can create a bridge between ourselves and our source.

Wow, that is powerful! I have spent my whole life working on my relationship with my higher power. It would be close and daily for some time and then I would grow distant again and the daily practices would end, and I would just live in my human world. But obviously there was a collective creation happening during the passage of time that allowed the opening that I've experienced over the last year to happen. This is what they want us to understand. To not get discouraged, because any work you do stays there. It doesn't disappear, it doesn't go away. You're using this lifetime to create this beautiful connection, one glistening thread of energy at a time!

Let it unfold and begin the puttering, the joyful puttering throughout your day, in between doing things that you feel like doing. Your days do not have to be spent all on spiritual endeavors. The spiritual endeavor of learning to have the conversations inside your head and trust that it is us, that is where you really are needing the most growth right now.

They are talking about the internal dialogue between them and me. I described, in my first book, that voice that I've always had. A voice that was different from my thoughts. But I didn't ever really trust it. During my spiritual awakening I learned to channel that voice. When I channel that voice, it comes through with a lot of energy that I can feel in my body. My jaw will shiver and according to the strength of the transmission, my body will shake, I will yawn, and I will twitch and flex.

3

Sounds great doesn't it, but it is validating! I know that I am connected when I bring through those transmissions. They want me to practice knowing I'm connected when I hear their voice in my head. That is very difficult to do! Because our ego and our left brain will get involved and confuse the crap out of us! They are asking me to practice asking them a question in my mind and receiving the answer. I'm working on it, but it's difficult.

This is how my book starts, with a conversation. This is going to be interesting! I believe it is going to be an unfolding as opposed to my last book. My last book was a very specific timeline. I went back to the beginning of my journey and told the story up to a certain point. That was straightforward. They are telling me that this book needs to be a different kind of experience. To be honest I'm a bit confused! But I have redefined faith and I know that if I follow the guidance, everything will turn out just fine!

Chapter Two

Vibrational Frequency

They are telling me that before I start my meditation, reach out and ask for the highest beings, for my highest good, to talk to right now. They say I don't have to be able to form the question, that they know and love me exactly as I am, where I am. And to just know, that I have access to vast, limitless amounts of support from the non-physical side. To just step back and let the message come.

The YouTube message that you watched this morning resonated completely with you. They spoke the truth of the evolution of humanity. We have given you that vision Kelly and it is the truth. Now you are expanding on that truth and your level of understanding of it. Every moment has limitless possibilities. The way that you define your next step, or the next unfolding, is by the frequency that you are in. The frequency of expectation, of waiting for that joyful, amazing thing to be right around the corner. So many of us on this side are coming through to those like you, with the message of how to be on the creative path for the highest good for each of you, and the collective you.

This is something they have spoken to me about many times. Standing in the present moment, with a true sense of knowing that wonderful things are on their way to you, is incredibly powerful. Everything is frequency. Every thought, every word, every action, rides on the vibrational or energetic frequency that it holds. We are learning to identify the frequency and bring it higher. The frequency of expectation, as they spoke of, waiting for that joyful, amazing, thing, is very high. Take a minute and close your eyes and think about that for a minute. Don't try to identify what might be on its way, the universe has far greater possibilities up its sleeve than you can even imagine! But take a moment and sit in that feeling of expectation.

Where do you feel it? Find it in your body, I feel it in my chest. On this journey together, we are going to learn how to identify and impact our frequency, our vibrational output might be another way to state that. All emotions have a vibrational frequency. Of course we know that the energy signature of love and joy are at the higher end and the energy signature of fear and hopelessness are at the lower end of the emotional continuum. What they are talking to us about is being able to intentionally impact where we are on the continuum.

We are coming through with a variety of messages trying to help the human species learn to utilize their creative ability. When we spoke to you yesterday about creating a system that would facilitate people to control their vibrational output, that is exactly what we were speaking of. You are thinking of the different processes and teachings that the Abraham group brought through, they did give lots of concrete things for people to do. We are speaking of something different. Be open without having to define it. Let us bring you along step by step and then you will be able to put it into a doable, attainable, way of living. That is what we are talking about. You get glimpses, for example the speaker on the YouTube channel this morning was calling it the five D perspective. Stepping into that vibration of the 5th dimension is the step on the creative journey that most human beings do not have the ability to grasp. You have an understanding already that humans are on many varying pathways. You understand that a human who is vibrating at a low frequency is unable to "hear" the words that are being spoken at such a high frequency level. The YouTube video spoke directly to your heart because that is where you are vibrating, at that higher level.

You immediately think that it is so much easier for you to attain that higher level of vibration because you can sit in the luxuriousness of your morning, without 1000 things to do. No job to go to, no kids to tend, no husband that is demanding, that makes it is easier for you to find it. That is absolutely true, it helps it be attainable. There will be those, like you who will resonate with the process and be able to attain the higher level. The speaker you listened to a few days ago, spoke of the rising tide raising all the boats, that is true, we are bringing through to you the processes that we want to bring forward to the earth, that will allow as many as possible to resonate with this higher vibration. To live life within that space, even as you speak of it, you can feel that space, that space of knowing, knowing... how do you maintain that space, you go into training Kelly, just like you did to learn how to be a medium. You opened the gifts along the path. The gifts are along the path for everyone. The various abilities that people can have, to be able to dialogue with non-physical energy, at any given time, is only one example.

There is no question that the busier a person is with the demands of life, the harder it is to tend to your vibrational output. Wouldn't you also agree that it is the most important time? You will learn techniques within this book that will help you to build that bridge to your higher self.

Take heart dear ones, you do it one small, glistening, energetic thread at a time. Each of you can find some time throughout your day to work to create this bridge. Particularly knowing that none of your work is in vain, it will collect overtime. But most importantly every time you consciously and intentionally set your vibrational frequency it raises the collective vibrational footprint of humanity.

They never cease to amaze me! I was dictating right along, and my jaw began to shiver, and I knew they wanted to speak. I didn't realize how this would work; we are all just along for the ride!

You asked us in your mind, as you put out the dogs, were we going to give you a process, a method, an attainable thing, that you could bring forward and teach? Yes, that is exactly what we are going to do. You are doing very well Kelly, listening to the voice in your head. It does seem odd to you to have such a back-and-forth conversation within your mind, but you are doing very well, and this is part of the journey.

Your first book will draw people to you Kelly because of your personality and the earnestness of your story. It will resonate with people, and it will bring them to you in a way that you cannot even fathom at this time. (I can't even imagine it!) *The next step is going to be to help people learn how to be in that vibrational state of <u>knowing</u>. That is where we want this book to go. For you to describe living this life, for you to tell your story and take them on a journey with the specific theme being the place of <u>knowing</u>. You feel a bit confused about this right now, that is OK, it will unfold, you do not need to see the timeline as it unfolds, you just live in your greatest joy.*

So let us give you some very specific instructions. You dabbled yesterday... a negative word or thought came into your mind, and you immediately acknowledged that thought. You said to yourself, "negative is not where I want to be, it's not where I want my vibrational frequency to be." So, you just closed your eyes and melded with your higher self. You dropped into your heart with love for humanity, love for the earth, love for your favorite pet, it doesn't matter what you sink into. You feel... the average person will feel the vibrational shift in their heart when they think about their favorite pet, when they think about that beautiful, giggling grandchild, whatever they can use that will raise their vibration. Then you are going to go into the rest of your day and the next thought will come and you are going to repeat the process. That is what you are going to practice. It will take self-control, and it seems simple to you, but it is how you bring yourself into that 5D consciousness, understanding that 5D consciousness.

I am going to be honest with all of you when I say I don't really understand what the 5D reality is, but I'm beginning to. We will learn together. Let's ask them now, what it is and see what they give us in real time… *You have asked us to explain to you and your readers what the 5D, or 5th dimension reality or understanding is. There are many resources available for you to explore your understanding of this concept. For now we will say it is a slight shift in consciousness from the third-dimension, concrete, linear 3D reality that you live in now that is governed by time and duality. The human consciousness is headed for an energetic shift. There are many dimensions dear ones, but at this time we are explaining the vibrational shift between the third dimension and the fifth. When you did the exercise that Kelly laid out previously and you dropped into your heart with that feeling of expectation, it redefined the present moment did it not? There was a slight altering of your consciousness. When you deliberately, with your intention, affect, or regulate, your vibrational output or frequency you are stepping into the power of the 5th dimension. It is that state of knowing that any wonderful possibility could come to you. It is the ultimate state of creation in a sense. As you all collectively influence the vibrational signature of humanity by practicing these techniques you are facilitating the way for the All. We know this is a complex concept for you to understand at this time, just know dear ones, that you are working with source energy for the greatest development of your planet.*

Holy cow that's kind of big! Every time I sit down to write over these last few days, they have changed the process. So, I'm just going to go with the flow! There is no question that humanity is undergoing a tremendous energetic shift. I believe that my guides, Lacroose, have an agenda. But I want to stress here that I always can exercise my free will. I feel that everything we can do to raise the energy, or the light on our planet is a positive thing. That is my greatest desire. No one knows better than me how "out there" some of the ideas that I will be sharing in this book are. I just ask you to take what resonates and leave the rest. Test this in your heart, that is one of the greatest lessons that my team bring through. We all have the gift of discernment, so ask yourself how does this feel...

So, let's move into our day practicing dropping into our hearts, or dropping into our consciousness and being in that place of anticipation.

Knowing, without a doubt, that our human brains don't have the ability to dream up something that is as fantastic as the universe can deliver. Asking yourself with childlike abandon, what could be around the corner? What fun, awesome, amazing thing is waiting... And when you feel that slight shift in your energy picture that beautiful energetic thread that you have created, that will never go away, that you will build upon next time as you create the bridge between you and your higher self.

Chapter Three

One, Two, Three

It has been several days since I have had time to sit down to write. Over those days I spent my time with my family helping my son and his fiancée work on their house that they are building. It is a huge undertaking and time has certainly slipped away from them in getting their foundation capped over before winter truly hits. I have consciously tried to put into practice what the Guides have given us in these first couple of chapters. You can imagine on a job like we were working on, there are many bosses and not very many workers lol! My son wants to be in control of this process, as he should be, because it is his house after all. But his dad is the one who knows how to build a house. It is always interesting to watch the dynamic between the 62-year-old father and the 36-year-old son!

The first day I found myself getting annoyed! There was lots of disorganization and wasting time as we chased our tails fighting the cold. It is November in Maine after all, the highest the temperature hit was probably mid 30s. So, sitting still was not a good thing, we needed to keep moving to stay warm. I must admit, I had periods of annoyance and frustration. The following morning, when I had a few minutes to myself to reflect on the success I had, or had not, experienced in being in control of my frequency the previous day, I let myself ponder my reaction to the day. As humans, when we can pull back and look at any given situation, like we are actors putting on a play, it is much easier to find the humor in the situation. I was able to ask myself "what does it really matter how organized we are, we are here to help, and we are helping, things are getting done, even if it's slower than it could be" I sat with that thought for a little while and then of course began to beat myself up for the frustration and low vibration that I had experienced the previous day. I tried to remind myself what Lacroose had said about letting go of the past and being in the present moment. That is a very hard thing to do. Let's ask Lacroose about the present moment...

Humans in general take themselves far too seriously! You chose to come forth to this planet for the joy and expansion that can happen in this 3D experience. This is a world of duality; the duality keeps people in a state of judgment. Humans look at everything in their life and determine, is this a good thing or a bad thing. Is this right or is this wrong, the journey through this lifetime is to work your way to the energy of Isness, or Beingness.

Humans, with their ego and their nature of needing to be right, to prove their worth in the world, create a daily paradox that keeps them from attaining their highest good. The ego does not want the human to own their power. The ego reaches into the past to remind the human of mistakes and problems and situations and this keeps the human in a vulnerable, weakened state. The ego is a vital part of the human, it is what creates the duality in a sense. Without duality, there are not the choices for the human to make consciously and intentionally. It is through those choices that the human has the potential to add to their connection to their higher self. We are using the example of the thread of energy that will build a bridge between us. That feels right in this situation, for this discussion.

Humans often ask why they chose to come to this planet. It is because without the ability to choose, without making conscious decisions to evolve, there is no growth. You are the leading edge of creation. You are incredibly powerful.

You must remember that you were born to this world with duality and the ego is the master of the absence of light. You can ask yourself, does any given thought subtract light from the situation? Is it a judgment? Does it in any way have a commentary about the past, thinking and rehashing what has come before. Spirit knows that the past does not exist, it has no bearing on today, you can as easily step away from the past as you can turn the pages of a journal. We are nudging you to look at the blank page and wonder, expect, dream all the wonderful, loving, happy, fun experiences that will go on that page. Does a thought lend itself to childlike wonder or possibility? If it does it is aligned with spirit. Does a thought make you to question or doubt any wonderful possibility... then it's from the ego.

Exceptionality is the order of the day. To live in the knowing that you are totally and completely loved and supported by non-physical energy, who has a broader perspective and can help guide you along the path, but you must ask. The human experience is one of free will, ask your angels to assist you in any endeavor big or small. Bring your guides into the smallest of undertakings, cleaning the house, having prayer time, going shopping... practice calling them in and watch the magic that will happen! When you get your answer, or a wonderful thing happens, acknowledge that you were supported, and it will get easier and easier.

You ask what to do when you see ego rear its ugly head. You step back, you observe it in the minute. You change your perspective from being it, to seeing it, then it will lose its power. Say to yourself "wow look at that" and watch the thought flow away. You might be tempted to say that it was ego, that it was bad! That is not the way, any judgment is of the ego. We don't judge, we love... take time every day to acknowledge how worthy you are. The entire angelic realm is very interested in you, loving you and waiting for you to reach out to them for guidance because you, right now, in this moment, are worthy, are loved completely, and you are perfect.

It all boils down to practice! Being willing to try. This is our life; we get to decide how we live it. We decide moment by moment what our experience will be. It is up to us to decide if we are going to live our life or is our life going to live us. Let's recap what they have given us today.

First, it's daily practice. Acknowledge to yourself that you have control over your vibrational output. Remind yourself that your vibrational output is creating your life. We create our life moment by moment either deliberately or by accident. The entire intention of this book is to raise the collective vibration one person at a time, because that is how it will happen. I know that in my life I have often thought, "what does it matter?" "I can't make a difference, after all I'm only one person living a very small life in rural Maine." But the reality is we all can make a difference! Own that knowledge, sit with it, let it roll around in your mind and in your heart, we all can make a difference! Because everything is about vibration. The more of us who are intentionally tending to our vibrational output, the more the collective will change and the brighter the future of our planet will be.

Second, be aware of your ego. They gave us very clear guidance on how to identify the ego and how to move past it. We need to practice that as well. I don't understand all the aspects of ego, but I do understand how they have explained it to us. Be consciously aware of your thinking. Our minds do not have to run all the time, we have control, even if it doesn't feel like it sometimes. The way we take control is to consciously interrupt our thoughts and ask ourselves if our thoughts feel good or not? Every time we do that, we are adding to our connection to our higher selves. Don't beat yourself up when you fail, we all are going to have that experience, just observe it, and let it float away.

And third, remind yourself of how loved you are. It's so easy to say those words but often very difficult to truly feel it. You are being told by Source Energy that you are perfect. Can you feel that in your heart?

Can you look out at the sky and feel your heart swell with the love that you know you deserve from God?

I wrote the beginning chapters of this book several months ago. I am currently more than halfway through the second portion of the book, which is the angels of the chakra component. This morning, as I was doing my personal meditations and spiritual work I had an epiphany. I decided I wanted to share it with you. Throughout writing this book my team has given me many different processes to facilitate living a spirit filled life. An ongoing question for me has been how do I remember? I will start my day centered and connected to my higher self, then I get busy, and I forget. They have told me many times that people like us, who are consciously trying, are raising the vibrational signature of our planet! Maybe it is my ego, but I want to do better! I have been trying different things to facilitate remembering to connect throughout the day. I want to share the fingernail story with you...

I was preparing to go away on vacation in January, 2023 and I wanted my nails to look nice. So, I spent weeks working with them. If you are like me and pretty nails do not come naturally, you know it takes quite a bit of commitment to grow them out! I had done well, and they were looking good. I had a gel manicure to strengthen my nails so they would last until vacation. I think it was three days after the manicure that one of my nails snapped off completely! I was so ******! I was out with friends, and I hate to admit it, but it did take some of the joy of my evening away because I was so in my head fretting about that nail! I went to bed that night and woke up the next morning, my first thought being about that stupid fingernail. Trying to decide, do I go to Lincoln and have a tip put on, do I cut my nails all off, it is silly, but I was spending a lot of time fretting about my fingernails... don't judge! I'm human lol and trust me I see the stupidity as well! At one point my broken nail caught my attention and I basically gritted my teeth in grumpiness when I heard a voice in my head say, "paint it red" and I said, "no I notice it all the time and I will notice it even more!" again my inner self said, "paint it red" and I said, "no! It's going to make it even more noticeable!" Then the knowing came, they told me that yes, you would notice it more often, isn't that the point? When you notice your nail Kelly, breathe into your heart, do the processes that we have given you, this can be your reminder! So, I painted it red! I call it my blessing nail. I now have a red thumbnail and a red ring fingernail, and the rest of my nails are long and have a French manicure! I'm going to wear it just like that on vacation to remind me that spirit is with me, loving me, and even interested in my silly fingernails!

Another epiphany about reminders that has come to me is about emotions. When we feel any emotion during our day, it can act as the reminder to come into our heart and use whatever process feels the best to you at the time. Any emotion, even the good ones, I think it's easier to bring yourself to your heart when you feel joy, but when you feel mad at a driver in another car it is harder, let it be the reminder to breathe into your heart. When you feel anxiety walking into a room full of people, let it remind you that you are one with God. Utilize the different processes that are throughout this book. In the morning during your spirit time, set the intention to be sensitive to your emotions, your emotions are communication from your inner child, as well as your spirit trying to get your attention. Let's set our intention to utilize emotion the way it was intended, as direct, back and forth communication between you and your higher self. It is the gentle tap on the shoulder that says, "remember you are loved." It is that reminder that you are creating your own reality, so where is your frequency right now? If your frequency isn't vibrating at a high enough level to attract into your life the things that you want, utilize the processes within this book to change it. It requires practice. I know that is frustrating, my guides have been talking to me about practice since the first day I channeled them! But what is life, after all, if not practice...

Chapter 4

Healing the Inner Child

I have always been a seeker. I've always had a very curious mind and wanted to know what made people tick. Throughout my life I have read dozens of self-help books trying to find the answer. They would often help for a while but then typically the teaching within it would fade away. When I would be reading any book, if it got to a section that discussed the inner child, I just skipped over it. To be honest I didn't really understand it. I would take the other parts of the book and that would be it. I always have spoken about having a toolbox. Things that I could dip into if I was feeling sad or upset about something. I had learned many tools over the years and have had great success with lots of them. But during the winter of 2020 my tools were letting me down.

We had been in a pandemic for well over a year and the stress and isolation were adding up. I was depressed and finding it very difficult to work my way out of it. I began some counseling which I highly recommend to anyone who is struggling, but finding the right therapist is very important! I was blessed with a wonderful woman who was there for me when I needed her. She gently guided me to this understanding of the inner child. With much research and reading and combining many theories and techniques, together with the guidance of my therapist I learned to understand and heal my inner child.

I want to take some time here and talk in detail about this process. It starts with learning about triggers. I thought I knew what triggers were, and I guess I did to a point. But my process started with identifying the reactions that were not completely from the adult perspective. I had listened to a podcast that talked about adult, adolescent, and child perspective. That really made sense to me. When we have a reaction to something that comes from any perspective other than an adult, that is the road sign that shows you something that needs to be healed. That is your inner child trying to get your attention.

I started using the voice memo feature on my iPhone. But you could use a little notebook to jot things down as well. To just acknowledge throughout your day when you have any reactions that are not what feel good. Jot down just a few details about what has happened and what you felt and then just move along with your day.

Each day I would take time for myself in the morning. Even as I write this sentence, I know that for many people that is almost impossible. But the fact of the matter is, to do this kind of work you have to prioritize it and give it the time that it needs. The payoff is living your life joyfully and deliberately not reactively and grumpy! In the morning I was in the habit of meditating. I would take out my phone and listen to several of the events that had happened throughout the day that had upset me. Then I would close my eyes and I would picture my little girl self. I would really try to see her, you can look at old pictures if that helps, ask her to join you up on your lap. Coax her, hold your hands out to her, make her feel wanted and loved as she crawls up into your lap. Allow her to stand away from you if is what she needs. You will feel if she doesn't want to come sit in your lap, and that's okay. Then from your adult space, filled with love and acceptance, have a conversation with your little girl about why she felt the way she did. My therapist was helpful to me in learning how to phrase things when I talked to my little girl. We use the same kind of therapeutic communication that we would use with anyone that we were trying to help. We empower the child, we don't tell them how they are supposed to feel. Honor the fact that they can feel any way they choose. But help them to know that they are loved and valued regardless of how they feel. I would talk with my little girl, and I would ask her to tell me what she was feeling. I would coax her along to tell me anything that she needed to say. I didn't tell her that she didn't need to feel that way anymore I just told her that I was here for her, and I had her back. I validated her feelings; I would say things like "anyone might feel that way" about whatever had upset her. I know this sounds strange, but I am living proof that it worked!

The truth is that many of us did not receive the parenting that we needed when we were children. Our parents all did the best they could (well maybe) with what they had to work with, and we are the result. When I started to make notes of the things that gave me that stomach clenching reaction, I began to see patterns. One of the biggest pattern was self-worth. If something happened during the day, something as simple as my boss asking me to come see him in his office at the end of the day, my stomach would churn, and my heart would pound. When I asked my little girl why that was, she told me it was because she was afraid she was bad. That she never did things right, and she knew he would be mad. I would have a conversation with her about her feelings. I would validate her feelings and tell her that I was here for her and that she was loved and could tell me anything. I would really let that little girl talk about what it felt like to be bad. To believe that people looked at her and saw her as bad. I would let her talk and talk and gently bring her around to challenging that belief. Asking her why would she think that people saw her as bad? She told me it was because they were angry when she asked questions, they were always shewing her away to her bedroom so they could enjoy the quiet. To her that meant she had very little value. So, we talked about how grown-ups often take out their own feelings on other people. How it was very understandable that she had come to the conclusions that she had. I explained to her she was loved, and how valuable she was and is. I would reassure her that I was a very strong powerful lady and that I thought she was perfect. I hugged her and stroked her hair and repeated over and over how good she was, how glad I was that she had come into this world, how much I loved her. I repeated that process often and still do.

I am quite surprised at my physical reaction to writing the above paragraph. Remembering how she felt is difficult. My parents were not bad people, they certainly loved me the best way they knew how, but a child is like a sponge, and they absorb everything that is going on around them and don't have the tools to know that it has nothing to do with them. This process might seem simple, but it is incredibly powerful. I was able to get to the point that I would use my drive to and from work to do this. I would turn my phone on after listening to whatever the issue of the day was, and I would record my conversation. I would title each conversation so I could go back and listen to whatever the topic was. When I told my therapist how I was using my phone she laughed and asked if she could recommend the process to her other clients!

I named my inner adolescent Darcy. The inner adolescent is the one who is always bitching about something! Never happy, always sulking, typical teenager! I began to watch my thoughts for signs of Darcy rearing her ugly head and I would find them! I started to understand that the grumpy teenager was there trying to stand up for, and protect the inner child. I found that as I nurtured and loved my inner child the grumpy teenager started to diminish. I've found it empowering to be able to identify the orientation of my thoughts. When my brain was running with a nonexistent argument, I knew Darcy was in her protective mode. I would ask myself what is going on really? What is the underlying fear that the inner child has that Darcy is trying to protect her from. I believe that when we learn to excavate what is behind our thinking, we can heal it and move beyond it. I got to a place where if my thoughts were running in that kind of a direction, I would say out loud if I could, "Darcy I've got this, I have everything under control, we are all safe and we are all loved, and you can trust me to take care of things." Often that would be enough to set me in a more positive direction.

It was incredible to realize how much of my day-to-day reactivity was a result of those deep-seated beliefs from childhood. I had a lady tell me once that we spend the first thirty years of our life being programmed by other people, the second thirty years undoing the programming and figuring out how we really feel about things. Then the last thirty, we get to live life as our authentic self if we are lucky. I believe that for our spiritual development, we must do some of the work to heal that inner child. That was the truth for me. I know that for myself the work I did healing my inner child was paramount to my awakening. I did not know for about 57 years how low my self-esteem really was.

Chapter Five

Relationship Between Frequency and Consciousness

You are asking for us to define consciousness. Consciousness is the one that knows that I am here. How do you know that you are here? You sit, you take a breath, and you sense, "here I am." But who senses? Consciousness is who senses. Consciousness is that second between thoughts. The observer, who can watch your life unfold. That is consciousness...

A huge concept on the road to awakening is defining consciousness? I went to a meditation class once and the leader of the class had us take our consciousness and move it up into the corner of the room. To observe from the corner of the room, and then to bring our consciousness back into our heads and observe from there. That is something worth practicing. Being in control of your consciousness is a very powerful thing.

What are we besides consciousness? We are all the things that make us who we are. We are all the labels that being human gives us. Wives and mothers, daughters, friends, whatever we do for a profession, we are all those things. They are all very much a part of who we are. All those things make up the story of you, and me. But those things are part of the play that we are acting out here on earth. They all add up to a specific understanding that stands between each of us and awakening and it is this "I am a separate individual. I have no power of influence outside of myself." That is a great lie, as I have written this sentence my jaw has begun to shake so I know they have something they want to say...

The illusion of separation is part of the human experience. You were born to this earth forgetting who and what you truly are. The goal that you have set for yourself as you come forward is to try to remember. You are part of the whole, part of the sea of consciousness, part of the All. You hold within yourself all of the abilities and gifts that you see around you. You believe that God, sitting on his great throne in the sky, has bestowed upon the rare individual the gift of mediumship, the gift of healing, the gift of channeling, and on and on the gifts go, but only for a specific few. That is the lie that you believe. For what you have forgotten is that all those things lie within you. Waiting for you to remember that you are part of All that is. You are one with everything and hold within yourself the power of it all. It is through this belief of separation, that heartache develops. The unrest and the disease that humans experience because of that belief dear ones, is because you are not intended to be comfortable within that belief. What drew you to this book? What drew you along the path that you are traveling to the desire to know who you truly are? That spark is within you dear one, that inner knowing that what you see on the surface of this world is not all that there is.

Every journey starts at the beginning, the beginning of your journey starts with the ability to feel love and loved. To learn to consciously control your vibration, your frequency. Your consciousness, that part of you that is one with non-physical, is beckoning you forward. The only moment that you have is now. All creative power is now. So intentionally drop into your heart and feel the knowing that we are beckoning you too. That every wonderful thing is possible. That you cannot even imagine how wonderful, wonderful can be! The universe has so much in store for you all, your part is to align with it. You do that simply by raising your vibration. Humans want things to be more complex! They want it to be hard with many steps and lots to ponder. But it is not difficult, think of anything that gives you that shift in your heart. You know what we speak of. When you think of that puppy, and your heart expands, that is the creative force of the universe. It might seem simple, but the rewards are anything but! Bringing this into day-to-day life, moment by moment, is the key to unlocking all potential, and all joy that life has to offer.

Understanding the relationship between frequency, or another way to say that would be our vibrational output, and consciousness is important, because if you are striving to become awakened, you want to be more consciousness than personality. Our personalities are all those things that make up the I. All the different roles that we play as humans within our life make up the story of our personality. I now understand that the goal is to be more consciousness than personality. When we exercise our deliberate intention to change a thought, drop into our heart and breathe in the love that is who we truly are, we are shifting from personality to consciousness. It is that practice that will lead us to freedom. Freedom from being affected by what goes on around us. Freedom to be joy amid sorrow. Freedom to love in the face of hate. Freedom to be or do or have anything in this world that we want.

This is the law of attraction. There is no question that our world works on this principle. What we give out is what we get back, no exceptions. My learning of the law of attraction was very empowering to me and I lived practicing the principles and processes that were taught by other beings that were channeled into this world. All of it resonated completely with me. I knew at some level that it was true. But it left me wanting more. For me, life was not all about getting the material things that I wanted. I had developed such a close personal relationship with God and Jesus, as a child and it was a wonderful blessing in my life. The dogma of organized religion left scars in my childhood that was part of what I needed to heal before I could move forward. What I'm speaking about now is combining faith in a higher power, the knowing that you have sentient beings who are helping you throughout your life with the power of the law of attraction.

That is why Lacroose is so determined to help us learn to control our vibrational output. Let's move into our day using anything that we can as a reminder to drop into our heart and feel that sense of expectation, wonder and love that connects us to all that is and brings all good things towards us!

I want to share with you my experiences yesterday after I finished writing chapters four and five. I felt off, it's difficult to explain but as I was moving through my day, I had this weird sense like I was doing something wrong, almost a guilty feeling in my chest and I didn't know where it was coming from. But I used the off feeling as a reminder to come back to the present moment. To drop into my heart and alchemize the energy into that pure, positive feeling of expectation and love. As I continued to do that throughout the day it began to lessen but when the feeling would settle around me, wondering if I was on the right path, I would ask my guides, in my mind "what is going on, why am I feeling this way". I realize that it has to do with control. When I wrote my first book, I thought **I** was going to tell my story. But very quickly my guides helped me to see that I was going to use a lot of my downloaded material. That made sense of course! Why wouldn't I share all the wonderful guidance that they had given me with my readers? As I would come and go to my writing of the last book, I felt a clear path. I knew exactly where I would pick up the next time I sat down to write.

That is not how this book is unfolding, I'm beginning to understand that they want me to chronicle my journey of living in this energy, of growing and evolving within this energy. The conversation between my guides and myself has mostly been out loud, dictating into my phone. When I do that, I get the physical sensations that validate to me that it is them. I'm beginning to understand that they want me to get more comfortable listening to them within my mind without validation.

Maybe better said, getting comfortable with them within my mind with whatever validation comes. My first book was a tool for me. I learned and grew so much, transcribing the downloads as I wrote about the impact they had on my life. I think the process of writing this book is intended to really help me embody the principles of living in the joyous present moment.

Chapter Six

Doing The Work

They stated previously in this book that they wanted us to learn together how to shift into that 5th dimensional vibration. The only way we can do that is from the present moment. Why are we so compelled to live in something other than the reality of the present moment? Our minds have certainly been programmed that way. Let's shine a light on what that programming is. It has been my experience that when I bring a pattern of behavior into the light of day and dissect it a bit, I am much more able to step away from any part that doesn't serve my highest good.

They are telling me that this goes back to childhood. Many, reading this book, will have come from a background where children were to be seen and not heard. Parents believed they needed to train their children to behave, to have good manners, to be respectful. I certainly understand the desire for all those things, but I wonder if the pressure of feeling responsible for someone else's behavior isn't what created the internal conflicts that many parents experience including myself.

Let's think about this from a parent's perspective. I imagine that most people who will be reading this book have been parents at one point. I remember having a lot of guilt as a young mother. I never felt like I could do enough. It always seemed like other women enjoyed their children more than I did. Don't get me wrong, I absolutely adore both of my children, but I was not comfortable when they were small. My husband would get home from work and get down on the floor with the kids and play. I would watch him, and my heart would be happy that he was doing that, but it also made me feel guilty because I didn't want to do that, during the day, when I was home with them. I don't know why; it just wasn't part of my makeup. It's making me very uncomfortable even to admit this but I'm feeling led to do so.

I would consider myself, even back then, to be an enlightened individual. I read books on parenting, any time I had a problem with my children I would research and find a solution that was brought forward by some expert because I certainly didn't trust my own instincts when it came to raising my children. If I struggled as much as I did, imagine the parents of 20 years before that, trying to do their best and not having a clue! We didn't understand the effect that energy had on our children. That our frustration and guilt was understood by them as a value judgment on themselves. Children develop the need to try to help mom and dad be OK. They learn that if they are funny, if they are very good, mom and dad act happier. So, this results in the child thinking that their worth is derived from their actions.

How would a person develop the ability to live in the present moment when all their training went into evaluating what you did last and planning what you were going to do next? And that it all rested on the reaction of someone else, not us. We were not trained to find the value in just being. We were not trained to know that we brought light into the world by our very existence. To be able to sit in the knowing that our actions have absolutely no bearing on our value. What an incredible concept!

In the first book, Lacroose explained that non-physical energy has no judgment of right and wrong, good or bad. I remember that they compared the relationship between humans and their non-physical team to be much like the relationship between a child and their parent. In that a parent brings experiences and challenges and guidance into the experience of the child hoping that it will help the child along their path. So does our non-physical team, the biggest difference, they explained, is that our non-physical team is never disappointed. This is a very difficult concept for us humans, me included, to grasp. But they have said it over and over in many ways. Duality, good and evil, only exist in the earthly plane. It exists to give us the opportunity to experience ourselves and find our way back to divinity. What humanity has forgotten is that when we are living true to our higher self, we are drawn to do loving, kind, things. We have forgotten as humans that we can trust ourselves. It is only people who are living their human experience so completely separated from their higher self, from that beautiful loving voice that we all have, that helps guide us to do things that we would label with our human judgment as bad, or evil.

I feel like we all need to take a bit of time and do the inner child process around seeing your value in just being. That is the only way we will ever find or have any hope of maintaining the present moment. Let's go into meditation and ask our little one to climb up onto our lap and ask them how they feel about being. Really listen, I am betting they will all have some distressed ideas about what that means. Let them describe it in detail, let them explain why they feel the way they do. What kinds of things did people tell them to make them believe the way they do? Who told them? What did they say? Let your little one talk as much as they can. Validate them, and just as if you were talking to a friend who was a child, with a child's understanding, help to bring them around to understanding their value. Asking them if they know that they are part of God. That God lives within them. All they must do is take their next breath on this earth to make the earth a better place. I encourage you to do this in some type of recording or writing exercise in a journal. I can tell you from experience that going back and listening, or reading is very helpful.

When we heal that perspective within ourselves, I believe finding the present moment and just dwelling there is going to be much easier. It all takes practice; my guides tell me this all the time! I get a bit frustrated to be honest, but I understand that it took a lot of practice to get me to the point that I am, or better said the point that I was a year ago. I have come a long way in my development and my understanding. However, I will be doing the above activity as well.

I just spent the last 20 minutes doing the inner child activity. I'm going to transcribe what I did. I hope it will be helpful, it is just to give you a guide, but I'm sure we all will have our own specific things that shaped us when we were little. This is what I recorded this morning...

Lacrosse, my team, my angels, I ask for your guidance, I ask for your help. As I heal the part of myself that is making it difficult for me to stay in the present moment. Thank you for showing me that this is what is happening. Thank you for holding my hand and guiding me as I have learned and grown so much over this last year. Help me connect to my inner child...

Come here sweet girl, come here Kelly Coleen, come sit with me on my lap. Come here pumpkin come snuggle right in. Yes, let me wrap this nice quilt around us both and snuggle us right in. That's my sweet girl. So darling, tell me what you're feeling.

LG (little Girl) I feel like I need to be good.

AK-(Adult Kelly) Well, is being good hard?

LG-sometimes it is, sometimes I just want to do my own stuff.

AK-What kinds of things?

LG-I want to play; I want to be down in my bedroom playing. I like talking with mom and daddy sometimes too, but I don't like it when daddy yells. And I don't like it when mommy tells me to go away. Or doesn't answer me when she's reading her book.

AK-she doesn't answer you honey?

LG-No sometimes I say her name over and over and she doesn't answer me.

AK-How does that make you feel sweetheart?

LG-it makes me feel like it I don't matter. It makes me feel like she doesn't like me, like she doesn't wanna be with me.

AK-What about when daddy yells, how does that make you feel?

LG-I get really scared I don't like it; I go down in my bedroom if I can. Sometimes I have to stay out at the kitchen table if we are having supper. I don't like that, sometimes we have things I don't like and he makes me sit and eat it anyway and I really don't like that.

AK-I'm sorry that that happened. I'm sorry you're feeling that way. When you think that your Mama doesn't like you, how does that make you feel?

LG-It makes me feel really bad, it makes me feel like I have to do something different, if I do something different maybe she will like me. I try to be funny, and I try to be cute. I try to make dad happy because I know when dad's happy it makes her happy, so I try to be sweet. Dad likes that.

AK-Do you sometimes act sweet when you're not feeling sweet?

LG-Yeah, I do quite a lot. Sometimes when I'm sitting on his lap, I want to get down and go play. But I have to stay sitting there until he tells me I can get down. I don't like that; I don't like him making me stay there.

AK-Tell me how you're feeling Kelly.

LG-I'm feeling uncomfortable, I'm feeling uncomfortable and weird I don't like how I'm feeling. My stomach doesn't feel right, I want to get down and go down in my bedroom. But if I don't act sweet and fun and happy daddy will get mad at me. So, I have to sit here and just be good.

AK-Sweetie, I'm awfully sorry that that happened and I'm telling you right now it's OK for you to get down out of his lap. You can get down and you can go right down in your bedroom where you feel safe. Wrap up in your quilt and get your cross and hang on to it because you know you feel like it brings Jesus close and makes you feel safe. Sweetheart you don't have to do what anyone else tells you to do. It is not your job to make daddy happy. It's not your job at all honey. I understand why you feel like it was because they made you feel like it was. I want you to know that your only job is to make <u>you</u> happy. The only thing you must do is just <u>be,</u> sweet girl just <u>be,</u> darling it's not your job to make anyone else happy.

LG-I don't think I believe you, because I think I'll be in trouble if I do something that makes someone mad, if I do what I want to do, and it makes them disappointed or mad then they're not going to want to be around me or love me anymore.

AK-Honey that's just not true, I understand why you feel that way but it's just not true

LG-But it is true because they get mad, and they yell and they stomp around and slam doors and then mum is upset, and she won't talk, and she just reads her book and smokes her cigarettes if dads not happy. I didn't feel safe. I didn't like it and I didn't feel safe. I just felt like I had to just sit there and be good until they had let me get down and go play.

AK-Honey you're safe now, can you feel my arms around you darling? You're safe now. You are safe and I'm here to take care of you. I won't let anything bad happen to you honey because I'm strong do you see how strong I am? Do you see how smart I am?

LG- I see

AK-I'm going to take care of you darling, you're just such a sweet, sweet girl and it's not your job to make anyone else happy, it's your job to make <u>you</u> happy. They all have their own responsibility to make themselves happy, do you see that sweetheart? Do you see that other people have to learn to make themselves happy and if they don't learn how to, then they're never going to be happy. But you can learn how to make yourself happy can't you pumpkin.

LG-I think I can. I just worry awful about making people mad or disappointed

AK-I understand you're worrying honey, but you don't need to worry anymore, you don't need to worry anymore.

LG-But what if someone gets mad at me?

AK-Well let's talk about that, what if someone gets mad at you?

LG-Then they're not going to want me to be around. They're not going to want me to be with them anymore.

AK-Well I can understand why you feel that way sweetheart. But you're never alone Kelly, you always have people right there with you. You have a whole team of people right around you. All of your guides and angels and brothers and sisters are all right there around you, loving you every minute, and do you know what I know for sure? I know that if you are just happy, just in yourself being happy, being who you are, it's like you are a magnet, did you know that? It creates you being a magnet and it brings all happy wonderful people to you, did you know that sweetheart?

LG-No, I didn't, all I have to do is be happy? Just me? And other people will be OK?

AK-They will, they will learn to be OK on their own, it's their own responsibility. It's not your responsibility honey, your only responsibility is to find your path to being as joyful and happy as you can be. Do you like the idea of that?

LG-I do like the idea of that! So, it's not my fault if other people are grumpy?

AK-No, it's not your fault honey, not at all. Everyone has a responsibility to take care of themselves. Everyone has a responsibility to act in whatever way that they're going to act, it hasn't got anything to do with you, people are weird sometimes, they want to blame us for what they do and blame us for how they feel, but that doesn't make any sense when you think about it does it? How is it your responsibility, as a little girl, to make a grown man or a grown woman act a certain way, it doesn't make any sense does it honey?

LG-No I guess it doesn't.

AK- And even in a grown-up's life, it's not any person's responsibility to make another person happy. It just isn't your responsibility it's their own responsibility. Our responsibility on this earth is to live true to who we are. To listen to that voice inside, do you hear that voice inside of you Kelly?

LG-Yeah, I do, it reminds me to say my prayers and makes my heart feel happy when I talk to God, and when I talk to Jesus.

AK-That's right that's because they are right there with you. You are part of them, you are part of the whole. You turn up the light darlin just by being you and being on this earth. You don't have to do anything. Even if you're in a grumpy mood, that's all right, you get to have a grumpy mood and then you just go to the next moment and maybe you're going to start to feel a little bit better because you're a magnet and every happy thought you think brings happy things to you. But it's doing the things that make you happy not doing things to make other people happy. Not that it's not fun and we enjoy doing good things for other people, but our purpose on this earth is to live our own happiness. To be in our own time in our own moment and thinking the thought that makes us the happiest in this moment, that's what our purpose is. So, you tend to how you feel honey, you tend to how you feel, your own happy thoughts, inside your own self. You just live your own life and if other people are grumpy or disappointed in something that you do, then that's on them, it's not your responsibility. It's not your responsibility to make other people happy. Yes, you can even disappoint people you can even disappoint them and you're still going to be OK because you are beautiful and perfect just the way you are. You are part of God, little one, you are God. Did you know that sweet girl? Did you know that you are part of God, and that God lives within you?

LG-I like the feeling of that, it feels good, it feels like when I pray, it feels so close

AK-That's right sweetie, you've always felt that beautiful connection and that connection is exactly where you want to be. That connection is the feelings that you want to feel, so remind yourself as often as you need to darling, that it is not your responsibility to make anyone else happy. They can have their feelings and they can work themselves through their feelings. It doesn't have to be upsetting, remind yourself that you can look at them, in whatever mood they are in, and you can just observe it. You can be removed from it, so it doesn't have any hurtful effects on you at all, just watch them like you were watching a TV show, and when you can just turn the station to a happier TV show. They will find their way to being OK and if they don't, then that is their life, it's what they have to learn. It is OK to just tend to your own happiness. You are so loved Kelly, you are so loved and so valuable in this world. You make light shine by just being. When you sit inside yourself and just find the love in your heart that you have, and you let that light of love shine out, it turns the light of the world up and that is a wonderful thing sweet girl...

I hope that was helpful to you, it certainly was to me! I didn't realize I still had so many feelings around that. This process is a tool for us all to have in our toolbox. I almost feel like when we heal these things, we heal levels or layers. Then we need to live with it for a while to excavate the next level.

Please remember that I'm not a psychologist, I'm sure the conversation could be worded in a better way to help heal that little girl, but this is what I must work with lol! I know I feel a lot better right now! Let's go into our day and practice our process. Remind ourselves with every moment of love and appreciation, to drop into our heart, to breathe deep and feel... Feel that feeling of anticipation, the feeling of knowing that we are a magnet drawing to us the next most wonderful moment that we can experience! Reminding ourselves that every time we do that, we turn the light of humanity up and it never is the same again! We are doing the work together!

Chapter Seven

Negative Emotions

It never ceases to amaze me how the universe gives us so many opportunities to learn and grow and develop in the way that we need to. I do not believe that no matter how enlightened anybody might consider themselves; we will be done having strong negative emotional reactions to things. How we deal with them, however, is what will change. The following is my morning download, it gives a clear example of what I mean.

This morning when I was watching my YouTube video with a woman who is 52 and has only been channeling a short period of time maybe just a couple of years. She already has created this huge business and is on this show being interviewed. I felt jealous, and I don't want to feel jealous. So why <u>did</u> I feel jealous? Why did I let that be a part of my morning?

Jealousy is an emotion that is on the lower end of the emotional continuum that we have spoken to you about. That is why you do not like how it feels, it is not part of what you are choosing, it is a vibration that is outside of your normal vibrational output. But you are asking why you felt jealous when you say you are happy with your life unfolding the way that it is. It goes to that belief, that internal belief, that child's inside belief of not being good enough. How is this woman better than you, that things have expanded in such a way for her, but not for you? That is part of the human condition Kelly. When those things come up in your life, acknowledge them as we have spoken of before. Bring it out and let the light of day shine upon it and it will wither and die. Find the place in your own heart, in your own being, that knows that things are developing for you exactly the way they should. We know the highest good, we know your heart, and you are having such glorious days are you not? Enjoying the process of writing book number two. Enjoying the process of watching as book number one goes out into the world.

It is easy as you click on that report concerning your book and yes, this morning it felt very much to you like stepping on the scale. You are measuring yourself against something. That success is measured by the number, and you know that that isn't true. The vision that we have dropped into your mind of the books being pebbles in a still pond, each wherever they are in the world, reaching the people that they are intended for, in whatever way it is intended.

This morning you are going to write about that place of wonder, knowing that the universe and all that the universe holds, is so much more able to design an outcome than the human can. The human imagination can be used as fuel for excitement, wonder, dreaming. It is not wrong for flashes of experiences to come across your mind. In that wonderfully, anticipatory state, you see for instance being on a stage, you see the interviews that might happen and being able to talk about your book and the process of writing your book and how much you would enjoy that. Those are all wonderful things, and they have the energy of growth and expansion and the energy of wonderful things coming. The practice is to see those things and then sit in the knowing that if your human mind can come up with that, what more might your team in spirit be able to come up with for you! It was a wonderful reminder this morning to ask the angels for their help. The specificity of asking, stating to the universe that you would enjoy this or that does not mean that you are tied to that exact example. It means that something that is a vibrational equivalency or better is coming. That is a powerful thing, to know that your angels are interested. They want to help you all realize your dreams.

"I would like to have someone come into my life that wanted to use their gifts to help my brand go out into the world. But even as I say that there is a vibrational dissonance that is there. I don't want to be about the money, and I don't want to be about the success. I want to be about living in this moment with such joy and such wonder and all the moments to come. Knowing that if this is all that happens, if living with such a wonderful sense of joy and anticipation, and the happiness that it brings is all there is, then so be it. I could have never guessed or dreamt up where my life is today. There would have been no dream, no ability to dream big enough that would have resulted in me being able to do the things that I can now do. Bringing forth these books, it is just so fun and exciting, and I love doing it. *So, live in love Kelly, the joys of your days as one after another come into your experience. You are asking what is that little thread of negative energy that is running in that for you. Can you give up the idea of your book ever being famous?* "Well, I can, but it's an exciting thought." *That is the positive energy Kelly, the exciting thought is the positive energy, the anticipation, the wonder around that. But then when you let the human ego grab on to the idea of your book and start measuring it against anything else, measuring it against numbers and growth and all of that, then the judgments come, the doubt comes, that is the thing you need to release. So, we say it again, can you release the idea of your book ever being famous?* "Yes, I can. But why do you keep telling me that it's going to be…" *You are missing the point dear one,* "well I don't get the point." Go *back to what you know. You are in this moment and there are limitless possibilities for the future for you. Infinite, dimensional timelines with an infinite number of future outcomes. Tend to your vibration in this moment and let that be the only thing that concerns you. Living in the present moment is the power, Kelly. You don't live in the present moment for what it might bring, you live in the present moment for the joy and the excitement and the fun of the present moment.*

They have shown me repeatedly this vision of a point in time with unlimited possibilities branching out in front of us. We have no ability to imagine how many ways our life can play out. They keep telling me that it is the vibrational frequency that this moment holds that creates the next moment. As my mind has opened to this new perception of reality, I spend a good deal of time listening to other channels and the various messages that they bring through. It is validating to see the threads in common between them all. They want me to state again that we have no ability to dream as big as the universe can make happen! When we really can own that statement, it gives a night before Christmas, when you were a child, kind of feeling. Having no idea at all what might be under the tree, no limitations, all dreams... That is how they want us to live our lives.

It just occurred to me that this is why most channels do not predict the future. Because we have free will. I just reread part of the download, the part where I was arguing with them about them telling me that my book would be successful. What they dropped into my mind is that it is all possible in this moment. If my energy changes and my focus goes wonky, then the chances are pretty good that I will not realize that dream. If I stay focused on the present moment, living my best life, then that and much more is on its way to me.

This download was very personal to me but of course they all are lol! I would say 90% of the time I honestly am not invested in what happens in the future concerning my book, or whatever, but this morning I happened on to the report feature on Amazon publishing that tells me how many books I have sold and how much I have made in royalties. Just writing the thought makes my energy change and not for the better! I think the reason that I had this experience and can share it with you, is for us all to realize this is an ongoing process. We are not going to have these epiphanies and then be able to live them consistently forever! We are human, we chose to come into this incarnation to experience life and to grow. I think they brought this through, to show us that we will develop a sensitivity to these negative threads of energy. That is what we want. If we are sensitive to the small threads of negativity and do whatever we need to do in that moment to bring them to the light of day, as they said, then the negativity will not have a chance to grow.

As humans we are programmed to face reality. After all, who are we to think that we deserve any better than what we have? However, what I have discovered is that the object of the game called life is to know that you are supposed to have anything that you want. To sit deliberately for a moment in time and tend to your energy, tend to the frequency that you are giving out. Not beating yourself up because you didn't do that great of a job in the last moment, or yesterday, or last week or last year... Owning the present moment. Claiming it as your own, consciously wielding the power that will bring the next great moment, teaming with possibilities, to you.

But more than the joy of the moment, more than the joy of the life that you will lead. You are contributing to the whole, the vibrational frequency of humanity. Knowing that, gives another level of motivation to keep us going. Every time we consciously adjust our frequency, we are adding to the vibrational footprint of everyone. Remember, once that beautiful shining thread of energy is released, it can never be taken away. We are creating, though thought, our personal bridge to our relationship with non-physical and the collective signature that will raise the consciousness of humanity to the point that we will change the world.

I want to explain the perspective of the universe being able to create more magnificent outcomes for us than we can even imagine. The first time they dropped this thought into my mind was when I was standing at my kitchen sink doing dishes looking out the window at my deck railing. Some years ago, I planted morning glories in my yard in various places, they tend to spread on the wind which is quite lovely. You will see them pop up here and there and I enjoy them so much! At this point in time, I was looking at the railing and some morning glories had planted themselves at the edge of my deck, they had climbed up to the top of the railing and were cascading down the other side making it so that when the blossoms opened, they were pointed right at me in my kitchen window, they were glorious! I can't even describe how lush the green leaves were, how bright and beckoning the blossoms were as they opened and closed with the sun's rising and setting. I remember standing there in awe, thinking there would have been no way I could have planted these, in this particular place, to make them look the way that nature did. That is when they just dropped this knowledge in my mind. Humans create within their own frame of reference, that is limiting, the universe has no limits. Most of us, when we dream big, are still dreaming within the realm of possibilities that we understand. So, trust in the imagination of the universe, that feeling of wonder is such a wonderfully creative force.

Chapter Eight

The Present Moment

My heart is so full of all that I must be thankful for! It was after Thanksgiving last year that my journey of awakening started. So many glorious things have happened over this past year, and I am so incredibly grateful...

Yesterday was Thanksgiving, things were different this year. We will be having our big family meal tomorrow and I will be cooking a prime rib. We decided to have friends over yesterday for turkey. I think I was feeling a bit off, not having my family around on the actual holiday. We made the decision to help everyone be less stressed. My son must share the holiday with his ex-wife and my future daughter-in-law must do the same thing with her daughter. It's a lot of running around and the poor kids are forced to eat two huge meals in one day! So, I thought it would be better to change the day and I still think it's a good idea.

This morning I am feeling guilty. I drank quite a bit yesterday. I didn't do anything inappropriate, but I did drink too much. I'm sitting here kicking myself and feeling bad. I know I do not want that energy in my present moment. I dropped into my mind as my husband was sitting beside me on the couch and I couldn't talk out loud with my guides as I often do. I asked them to help me figure out why I was feeling the way I was. They reminded me that they absolutely do not care what actions anyone does. They are focused here with us, in the present moment, urging us to feel the love that they have for us. When I tried to talk to them about what I should have done differently yesterday and that maybe I could do different on Saturday when the family is over, they settled on me a knowing. Reminding me how many times they have told me that they do not care! You cannot disappoint non-physical. The only thing they have any concern about is the present moment. How can you make the present moment better?

As this book is unfolding, I see that they are trying to coax us into having a true understanding about the power of the present moment. Rooting out the cause of why our behavior is the way that it is can be helpful. I believe that is why they led me to include the section on working with my inner child. I want to state again that it had been months since I had done any inner child work. This morning as I was feeling guilty, I asked if I should think about this through the eyes of my little girl. The conclusion that I came to, is that I didn't like it when my parents drank when I was little. Things would often change and get grumpy. But I didn't change and get grumpy yesterday. I think this guilt around drinking is a habit. One that I need to let go of. I have spent so much time in my life beating myself up around drinking that I think it's just part of me now. Any thought or behavior that is not serving us can be challenged. I'm not saying that it is not good for us to moderate any behavior, what I am saying is, that sitting in self judgment is probably one of the most negative forces in our lives. They want us to know how loved we are. It astounds me, as I sit here trying to wrap my mind around what they are telling me, what they've told me many times before, that I do not need to do anything to earn their love. The love of God is based solely on my existence. What a wonderful thought, as I write these words, I feel a soft vibrational hum in my body almost like they're giving me a hug. Let's ask them for a tool that we could use when we are beating up on ourselves...

You have asked us to settle into your mind a procedure or technique for the human to release self-judgment. See it for what it is, when you have the voice in your head that is scolding and giving you heck about something, recognize it as that inner parent. The inner parent is the voice that is created when you are very young and joins with your ego. Your ego loves the inner parent because it keeps you weak. When you start to get your spiritual or emotional feet under you with any kind of security the ego/inner parent/inner critic rears its head and begins to undermine the work that you have done. You are asking us what to do at that moment. The ego mind is a tool that humans possess to facilitate their life on earth. It is needed, it is the part of you that assists you in the day-to-day functions that need to happen for survival. What has happened over your evolution is that the ego mine has taken the front seat, the driver's seat so to speak, that was never the intention. The soul mind, the part of you that sees the world through the eyes of source, is supposed to be in the driver's seat, but it must be invited. When you find yourself being driven around by the critic or the ego, invite your higher self into the driver's seat. Do it consciously with intention. State in your mind for the critic to get into the back seat and stay there! Invite with gratitude and love your higher self into the driver's seat. This sounds simple we know but you must practice doing exactly that when those negative, self-berating thoughts come. You consciously remind yourself that there is no perspective from across the veil that is judging you. You have the choice to remember that every time you consciously challenge the ego mind it loses power, you are closer and closer to winning! Congratulate yourself when you do this. This is what we mean when we talk about bringing something out to the light of day and shining the light of love and knowing on it. These things will begin to wither and die when they are denied constant attention. This is not an easy thing, for that negative voice is a much more comfortable voice, you have lived with it all your lives.

Practice your mind being quiet, being a place of love and gratitude. This is why positive affirmations have so much power. Because if you can focus your mind on a positive statement, it gives the monkeys something to do lol! Humans often call that running mind the monkey mind! We think that is an accurate description! Let's keep those monkeys busy in the workshop of your mind creating positive self-image. Reaffirming to you the love that the universe has for you. Let them set the intentions for the glory of your day ahead. This is the work they should be doing.

Let's break this down even further. We like this process. When humans identify the negative train of thought that has taken over their mind. It is likely that they are acknowledging it because they are feeling very bad. That is typically what gets your attention. The heavy feeling, the sick feeling in your gut, that familiar guilty, negative feeling that you are so in touch with. You practice it all the time, which gives it strength and allows it to grow. Identify that you are in this state with the ego mind happily driving the car at incredible speeds with the top-down whooping it up! We are giving this one a very clear picture in her mind of what that would look like. We invite you as well to use the visualization power of your mind to picture that. As the car speeds around with such joy and abandon knowing it is creating exactly what it wants to create, we see behind it rows and rows of monkeys with their hands in the muck. Their heads bowed, looking sad as they tried and tried to smooth the rutted muck that the car had created.

Bring that car to a stop and boot the driver out! Turn to your team of monkeys and direct them to go to the beautiful crystal-clear pond that is just up ahead. Direct them with love and care knowing they have not wanted to be working in the muck, but they had no choice. Guide them to the edge of the beautiful pond and allow them into that water, give them encouragement and love as they stand at the edge and wash their hands. Or plunge into the water frolicking and splashing as it cleans all the muck from their skin. Then notice what the monkeys look like when they come out of the pond joyful and clean ready to get to work creating the mindset of joy and anticipation and self-love. If you choose *to engage your mind in this way it will give enough time for the momentum of the negative thoughts, that car speeding around, to come to a halt. You do have this power dear ones. You have the power to direct your own thoughts. The ego mind works very hard to convince you otherwise. This is but an easy example of a process you can do that will help you readjust your vibrational output within the present moment. That, dear ones, is all you need to think about! There is nothing more important than to tend to your vibrational output, the frequency that you are living this present moment in. When that inner critic tries to tell you that you have done something wrong, send that monkey to the pond to wash away that thought because there is no doing <u>anything</u> wrong.*

You are asking about the people who do the atrocities. We have spoken to you about this before. If humans have allowed that ego mind to take full control, then perhaps they will make choices of harm and chaos. It is up to that individual to find their way back to their inner voice. Many do not think that is just the truth. But when they cross the veil, they will take all that their soul has learned living in the darkness, and it will be part of their experience when they come back and try again. There is no judgment dear ones. Your guides and teachers in non-physical work with you to make the trip as easy as possible. You choose to come into this world to learn and grow. If you are reading this book and trying to apply the words within it, you are on the right path.

You are asking if there is more we would like to say this morning. We would simply draw your attention to how you are feeling Kelly. Do you feel the sense of love and knowing that has settled around you? That is the work dear one, to go from feeling the way you did when you first woke up and you were experiencing guilt and self-judgment, to coming into the present moment with a clear understanding of how incredibly loved you are and that everyone on this earth is. We love completely those who are so far away from us that they cannot hear us at all. That is difficult for you to grasp we know. But it is true nonetheless, there are none of God's children that are not loved. You were trained as very small children to believe that what you do was what created your value. It is not about what you're <u>doing,</u> it is about your <u>being</u>. Your value comes from your sheer existence.

You do not "please" non-physical any more by doing what you would consider to be a good work, than by doing what you would consider to be an atrocity. Even as we give you this it does not set easily within your mind. We understand the difficulty that you have. Because you judge all things. You judge everything as either good or bad, right or wrong, that is absolutely the human condition. The path to enlightenment includes the understanding that duality is an illusion.

"I don't understand what that means"

We are showing you within your mind a movie playing out. When you watch a violent movie and it is done well, the human feels many of the emotions that the characters within the movie are experiencing. Is that not correct? But when you can step back with your intellect you can remind yourself that the movie is not real. They are just people playing out roles to evoke a response, and emotion from the viewer. That dear one is exactly what life is. "Holy crap this is getting deep" *To be able to sit in the space of observing without judgment, without any emotional response. That is the path to enlightenment. Knowing and trusting that each actor on the stage, so to speak, has learned their role perfectly and are acting out their part to perfection. It is a lot to grasp dear ones, but you are beginning to see the picture. The "reality" that you watch on the news has no more ability to affect you and your emotional output than if you were watching a movie. It is only that you can state within your mind when you were watching the movie to give yourself comfort "this is not real" use that dear one within your life. For it is no more real than the movie on the screen.*

You are confused, and they bit overwhelmed by what we have given you this morning. This is understandable. You are asking if life is no different than watching a movie what is our purpose in it? Your purpose is to find your way to joy. Your purpose is to be able to remove yourself from any reality and know that a higher power is watching with the same nonjudgmental observing that you are striving for. In the beginning of this book, we spoke about you all having the ability to affect the vibrational signature of your planet. This understanding is an integral piece of that puzzle. If you can maintain your vibrational output on the positive end of the emotional scale, you are serving humanity. It serves humanity, when you are on the highest end of that continuum of emotion, being in the vibrational vicinity of knowing, joy and anticipation. You might be in the vicinity of curiosity, even if you are only able to make yourself comfortable turning away, you have accomplished a positive thing. It all goes back to tending to the present moment, because the present moment is all that you have. The present moment is where your power is, all of your creative ability stems from the present moment.

Chapter Nine

Alchemizing Energy

The following is a download from July 26, 2022. I had had an uncomfortable interaction with my son Cory and was left feeling upset and so I went into meditation to talk to my guides. This is part of what they gave me. I want to include it because it is a helpful technique.

You asked us about your interaction with Cory this morning. You know that the words that you spoke were true and that you were not being unkind. There was no unkindness Kelly and yet your empathic self struggles a bit with that energy that he put off. That is the energy that you are feeling, you aren't feeling your own, you are feeling his and you are feeling Casey's because they are having their time as a young couple which is part of their path and their work, that they must do at this time. It was correct to speak the truth, it would be no less correct to have just sat and listened. You ask if as a mother should you in some way be required to tell him the truth. As you say that you are thinking the skill of reflecting back to him and facilitating him to come to his own conclusions might have been helpful. There are ways that are a bit gentler than just the truth. We feel in you that this is where you want to get. To the place of being able to stand in the truth. The place of connection, is the place of being able to observe him telling himself those lies without judgment. The piece that you are feeling uncomfortable with this morning is the fact that you were very harshly judging him. You are doing a good job learning this, fine tuning, you are fine tuning the human compulsion to, in some way, tell someone else what they need to do. To give advice, to help fix something that you see in someone else that you consider to be broken. Remember that the universe sees it all as perfect. Yes, every bad thing that is going on, there is perfection in it. That is making you feel a little confused. Remember there is no judgment on this side Kelly of good or bad. Remember that the souls that are in the people suits have lived many times. The soul is never hurt. The soul is never damaged. It is the pattern, in the human condition, that is creating things to be the way they are. It is up to each individual one of you to make decisions like you are this morning. You had the interaction, there was nothing wrong as such, you were not unkind. But you were not gentle either. You are looking at yourself, deciding for yourself how you choose to be. The more aligned you are with source energy the more you will be able to feel it when things are out of alignment. The interaction was out of alignment this morning and then repeating it to Michael caused him upset as well. None of that feels good to you. Don't judge yourself, you are learning from it, and you did well to not interact any further until you had worked some of this through in your mind.

You are asking about the conflict between standing up for yourself, standing up for your rights and being enlightened. These are human terms, being aligned with your higher self, that is where you want to be. There is no fixing anything Kelly, there is no apologizing. You can be immune to the pain and the negativity and the hurtfulness of others. You can be immune when you are able to rise above it and remove yourself from it emotionally. To be able to step back so to speak. Pull in your loving energy, the wall of love, just pull love in tight around you and love will protect you from anything that does not serve you at any time. You are making great progress. Think of the words that you spoke just recently, that every time you help somebody else you are basically taking their practice away from them. Had you just listened to Cory without comment, it would have spoken more to him than any of the words that you spoke.

They were right, if I had been able to just sit quietly it would have been so much more powerful. Silence can convey a lot. You are giving the person your attention and holding back judgment just allowing them to share whatever it is they want to share. People typically are looking for validation. You hold back the validation and send love, just replace it with love. I might have used sentences like "that certainly is a lot to think about." That would have made him think about things a lot more than any words that I could have said or advice that I tried to give. It is very difficult to hold back sometimes but certainly the ability to just sit quietly and listen is very valuable.

It doesn't have to hurt your heart; you can alchemize the energy into love. You are asking how you do that. The crystal that is in your heart is the spark of your higher self. It reaches in all directions; it reaches all the frequencies as high as you will allow it to reach. If you will settle into that during those times when things are uncomfortable, and you breathe into that crystal and you just expand that crystal in all directions, any of the energy that is not serving you will go into the beams that are coming out in all directions and go to where they can do the highest good. Perhaps they will feed the trees, when you breathe in, you also breathe in the power of the earth, the power of the four corners, you breathe into your heart. When you breathe out you are sending it to where it needs to go, and you are trusting the universe to know exactly where that is. When you are breathing in all the energy from the four corners, the highest frequencies that you can reach come into your heart. All the energy from Mother Earth comes into your heart. When you breathe out you trust that it all goes to exactly where it is supposed to go, and only the highest good will be left behind. Only that which serves your highest good will be left behind. Breathe in all from the four corners and all comes from the earth, breathe out, it is now transformed. You can breathe in any negative energy, at any time. You breathe it deep into your heart with your intention reaching out in all directions, the four corners and deep into Mother Earth bringing Mother Earth's energy up into your heart space at the same time you breathe it all in. You bring that all into that heart space and then you breathe it out transformed into love and kindness and compassion. That is alchemy, that is transformation. You are fighting against negative energy trying to hold it away, instead breathe it in with your intention hold it within your heart to be transformed for just a second and then breathe it out and it will go to the four corners and to Mother Earth to give exactly what is needed.

This is a tool for us to use to help us navigate the world and the negative energy that is around us. Prior to this download I would try to do a variety of things when I was around anyone who was giving off negative energy. Being an empath makes you very sensitive to other people's moods and behaviors. I did a variety of things that I still do on occasion as well. Such as putting a bubble of white light around myself, maybe having roses growing on the outside of the bubble to absorb any of the negative energy. I was able to picture a waterfall between myself and the person so that as the energy tried to get to me the waterfall would take it down into the earth. And all those things did help somewhat. But we know that what we resist persists! I believe that what they are telling us here is to take a more proactive approach. In my journey of learning about energy I had a meditation teacher tell me that when we cleared a room, we could send the negative energy out to the trees, and it was like manure, it would help feed the trees and help them grow. One of the things that came through to me with this download was that if God would give Mother Earth the ability to alchemize energy then why wouldn't God gave us the ability to alchemize energy? What they are basically telling me is that is exactly the truth and we do have that ability. Remember not to resist and push against, but to breathe it in and with our intention and with our strength of mind, alchemize it and send it back out to the four corners.

I wanted to speak to this concept of the four corners as well. This is a visual that they have used with me from time to time and it basically means that each of us has an ability to reach our frequency out. It speaks to the outer limit of our reach, and that that ability does change. It is affected by how high we are vibrating at any given moment. So basically, today when we consciously reach out to the four corners it might be a very different place that we are reaching than we did yesterday. The work that we do, those threads of light energy that we are working to create as often as we can, go into our vibrational offering and effects our vibrational reach. I think that the more tools that we have to deal with our day-to-day lives the better! This is a tool that can be very helpful. Do not underestimate the need for the energy from Mother Earth to come up into your heart as you breathe in as well. They showed me in my mind's eye energy coming up from the earth, and energy coming from all directions as well as from whoever or whatever situation is creating the negative energy. As you breathe in you are mixing all three of those things, cosmic energy, earth energy and the energy that we want to change. Mixing it into a cosmic soup with your love and intention creates a new vibration!

They have also shown me the importance of breathing in the beautiful, positive energy as well. When something happens in your life that gives you that beautiful, expensive feeling in your heart, breathe it in. Then breathe it out to the four corners, securing it within your heart and sending it out in all directions, to Mother Earth, to the cosmos, in this way we are adding to that vibrational signature.

Chapter Ten

Working With the Tools

We enjoyed a long weekend with friends and family over this Thanksgiving holiday. It is Sunday morning and I'm looking back over the last few days, surprised that I managed to fit in little bits of writing here and there. The way this book unfolds is quite remarkable, for instance, this morning I have been thinking about how I have applied the tools and techniques that they have helped us to develop within this book to my life. I have wonderful friends and a lovely family, however when you mix that all together for multiple days in a row you do tend to get tired! My favorite process so far is the monkey mind process.

Yesterday as I was preparing for my family's arrival, I cooked, straightened things out etcetera. My brain would occasionally grab onto some idea, some grumpy nonsense and take off on a tangent. I am a highly visual person. I would very quickly picture the monkeys rolling around in the mud, throwing mud at each other, being mad and grumpy. Then I would imagine other monkeys over in the pond frolicking and playing and joyful... It was like the happy monkeys would call to and splash the grumpy monkeys and the whole process would make me giggle, which of course served the exact purpose that it is intended for. I've begun to think of it as a click on a dial, every time we can interrupt that kind of negative train of thought we click our dial towards joy and happiness. Away from the internal arguments and judgmental trains of thought, that rear their head all too often.

This is our purpose in life. It's so simple and yet it's so profound. I took a moment at one point and looked around the room full of people and thought to myself that each individual person is somewhere along their journey to enlightenment. This was not a value judgment, only an observation. And it just struck me, that with all the hoops we jump through in life, with all the self-imposed shoulds and shouldn'ts, the sole purpose of life is to find your way to the present moment and be as high on the emotional continuum as you can be. Not judging where you land, just acknowledging it, knowing that you are striving for the next click on the dial, that will take you closer and closer to that place of joy and knowing, and anticipation.

Chapter Eleven

Our Relationship with Ourselves

I have mentioned before that I was born a seeker. Since the time that I was very young I have read books and asked questions trying to discover myself. I would often come across the term self-love. I found it a difficult concept to truly grasp. I mean think about it, to love oneself, of course we do, or do we? The summer that I did my counseling I had many personal revelations, but I would describe my understanding of the concept of self-love as happening in layers. I want to share this with you because I feel that it was an integral part of my journey. I still need to remind myself to practice what I've learned. I know how important this concept is for me to share, but as I sit and stare at my computer I seem to be at a loss. Let's ask the guides to define and help us with our understanding of the concept of self-love.

You have asked us to discuss the concept of self-love with you. This sounds like a cry from the heart, that we hear from so many of you walking the earth. It seems so simple to us and yet the human condition lends itself to self-sacrifice, or self-centeredness and the list would go on, but self-love seems to be something that eludes the average person. This one has often thought to try to see herself through the eyes of source and that is a wonderful perspective that might serve you. So, let's begin with that. What does it mean to see yourselves through the eyes of source? Look at an extension of oneself, for that is what you all are. That is difficult for you to accept we know, however, it is the truth. You are an extension of God. You are part of the All, the creative consciousness that makes up everything. That is who you are but you have forgotten. We understand, but it is the essence of the human experience. You come forth into the world and you forget everything that you are and you spend your time experiencing the world, striving to find your way back to remembering. That is the object of the game, so to speak. So to see yourself through the eyes of source, you see greatness, you see perfection. In the same way that a child is part of their mother and father, made-up from the stuff that makes them, that too, dear ones, is you. So that is one perspective for you to consider. But we generally find that it is one of the most difficult perspectives for you to embody.

I know what they are saying is very true but I wonder why? Why is it so hard for us to love ourselves the way that God loves us? When I think of how much I love God it overwhelms me. My heart feels so full and so expansive. It has been that way since I was a small child, the first way it was ever explained to me was at church when they talked about the Holy Spirit. I felt that Holy Spirit so strongly so overwhelmingly, that it sometimes felt like it would burst out of my chest, so much love... If I, as a simple girl, could hold that much love for God, and I am an extension of God, why can't I love myself that same way. The answer to that question is that I can. This is part of our remembering, this is part of the journey towards enlightenment.

That is right dear one, that is exactly right. The energy of that love is an incredibly powerful force. There are many reasons that the human find to not turn that love inward and that is much of what we want to cover in this book. We have already spoken to you of some very complex ideas. Living in the 5th dimension, with that kind of expansive view of the world, is the goal that we are helping you towards. Personal work and development is a very important part of that path. It is all about perspective. That really is the key to life. We speak to you of the present moment often, for that is the only point of power that you have. There is nothing greater that you could accomplish in the present moment, then do sit and basque in the love that we are discussing. This one has learned throughout her journey to do mirror work. She looks herself in the eye in the morning and smiles at herself and might wink and share that moment of joyful anticipation. This is a wonderful habit to develop. Humans sit within themselves and they look out and they spend a great deal of time working on their relationship between themselves and what they perceive to be the outside world. We want to remind you that that is an illusion. There is no separation. We are all one. It is so easy for humans to look into the face of a baby and have their heart swell with love and nurturing energy, we are challenging you to look into your own eyes with that same feeling. This has been said to you all many times before but we will continue to say it until you can embody it. So let us speak of some things that you can practice, yes there is that word again, but you must practice.

Mirror work is an incredibly powerful tool. We have given the inspiration around this technique to many, who have written books and such. Your perception comes from within to without. Your consciousness is housed within this body that has these eyes and these senses of perception. It is such a small portion of any person's day that they might glance at a reflection and acknowledge the individual that they are. But that dear one is vitally important. We have spoken to you of consciousness. It is the consciousness within you, that in this very moment, if you picture yourself up in the corner of the room looking down at yourself, that is consciousness. Your consciousness is not limited to the human body. Your consciousness is that part of you that is one with everything. The atoms that bind together to form all things upon your earth, are all vibrating, there is no separation the separation is an illusion. But you have been given a human body, and that human body is the mechanism through which you experience the world. It is where the eye begins to be developed. The separation begins, you look down at your hand and you see where it ends and whatever you are touching begins and you see them as two separate things, two separate entities, but that is illusion. Sit with that truth a moment dear ones, the oneness. We know that those who will be drawn to a book such as this already has so much love in their heart for the world. So much love in their heart for what they perceive as God. But also many of you have forgotten to have the love in your heart for yourself, because you have forgotten, that this being, known as you is one with everything, is one with love itself. What can we say, dear ones, to help you understand this at last. The love that you feel for God, in what you perceive as heaven, swells your heart and brings a tear to your eye, that is also the love you should feel, when you look upon this vessel that carries you through this experience on earth, at this present moment.

You have been taught from the time you were very, very little ,that one is better than another. This is not a concept that people want to admit, however it is the truth. Your world is so full of information at this point in time, everything is at your fingertips. But so much of the information that is at your fingertips is skewed to make you feel less-than. We all understand the mechanism and thinking behind advertisement. There has never been a time in your history that people have been subjected to such a barrage of information that is, at its root, meant to undermine your confidence in yourself. After all, you must judge yourself as lacking to need the many endless products that are out there. Just this one simple concept would be enough to make people feel flawed. Add to that what we have already spoken of, the parental relationship creating so many concepts within the child that they bring into adulthood, it is no wonder that you struggle to love yourself. We have spoken before that intention is incredibly powerful. We think of all the things that Kelly has set her intention around and even as she is bringing through this message she knows what we are going to say. There are many intentions to serve others, to be the best version of herself she can be. To not be judgmental, to be compassionate and kind. But what about setting the intention to turn all of those attributes inward. What does it mean to be kind and compassionate to yourself?

I am remembering a time this summer when I was meditating and I had a lot of housework and chores that needed to be done. I asked them to give me energy and help me to have a good heart and mindset, as I did the work I needed to do. They asked me, what would it feel like to have a dear friend stop by and look at me and say, "I want you to sit right there Kelly, I'm going to clean your house for you. Because I love you so much and I think you're so special and you deserve the sun and the moon!" So I sat with that for a few minutes and I really thought about what they were saying to me. Who should love me anymore than me? I thought about the perspective that I would have if I were at a friend's house who needed some help. How joyful and happy I would be as I did dishes and laundry and cleaned floors. I would be joyful and happy because I would be doing it for someone that I loved and I wanted to be helpful. That is what they were telling me to try to feel about myself. Have that feeling as you clean the bathroom or do your laundry, that you are doing this for someone special, someone who deserves the sun and the moon! It puts such a different feeling in my heart and gave such a lift to my spirit as I went about my day doing those same chores that I would have done anyway. But I played the game in my mind that I was doing this all for someone special and it just made such a wonderful day!

Yes, dear one, that was a wonderful perspective that we dropped into your mind this summer and you have practiced it often! It is so easy for you all to do for others and yet so difficult to do for yourselves. Again it goes back to childhood, we know we are beating this drum often but it is something we really want you to understand. You were taught to use your actions to affect the people around you. That it was important that you behaved in a way that would make this one or that one happy. It put that responsibility for care to the outside of you, instead of the inside, where it belongs. Think of the kind of world it would be if you all cared for and loved yourselves. When your emotional tank is completely full, you have so much more to give to the people around you. Your motivation comes from happiness and well-being instead of from self sacrifice and bitterness. So bring self love into your present moment dear ones, and know that it is a vital part of your journey to enlightenment. When you tend to yourself you are tending to your vibrational output and as we have said before, that is tending to the vibrational signature of humanity. That seems incredible to you, we understand, but it is the truth. If you feel judged for taking care of yourself, look at the person who is judging you and ask yourself if that person took care of themselves today? Or are they looking to you because that is their habit. Though it is human nature to feel guilty for not doing everything for the people around you, you are undermining their ability to take care of themselves. It makes the human incredibly vulnerable when they are dependent upon others and circumstances for their well-being. When you can find your own state of perfection, within your own self, that is when you are knocking on the door of the 5th dimension.

I remember the Abraham teachings would say that a person could be so free that they could choose bondage. I didn't really understand that until right this moment. I think they are leading us to a place of being so content in the present moment that it simply doesn't matter what is going on around us. To be in a place of such security and such knowing, that you know the next best thing is just around the corner so you are not concerned with what is right in front of you. To be so grounded in your faith, that if you were to receive the diagnosis, you would immediately know there was something for the highest good coming to you as a result. It may be coming to you or the people around you I'm not sure... What a wonderful place to live that would be. I feel like they are working closely with us trying to help us attain that level of peace. Because that is truly what we are talking about aren't we? The peace of knowing that no matter what is going on around us we are absolutely OK wow...

I wrote Chapter 11 six or seven weeks ago. This morning, my guides wanted me to come back into this part of the book and explain another perspective. Our spiritual development and awakening will never end. As we develop layers of understanding and we become comfortable at that level, it creates the space for the next level to come in. I experienced that this morning. They had given me this perspective of interacting with myself in the third person months ago. I have used it and it works! That idea of being your own friend, your own champion, your own caregiver. The perspective of doing things for yourself like you were doing them for someone else, that you really loved, opened my eyes to an aspect of self-care that I did not understand up to that point. Today they built upon that. They drew me to a YouTube video by Terra Arnold that was wonderful! The name of it was **Finding Your Inner Child - How To love Yourself - Key To Joy - Ascended Masters Guided Meditation.** After I listened to that video, I knew that it was the next layer of understanding in my journey to self-love and I wanted to share it in my book. Cultivating a relationship with your inner child is very important within your spiritual growth. I learned that in the summer that I did my counseling before my awakening. This brought it to a new level of understanding though, a more personal, real perspective. To have a daily relationship with that beautiful part of yourself, including her, nurturing her, playing with her. That is a huge step in your personal development.

Chapter Twelve

Connecting With Your Guides

As I have been led to title this chapter I realize I have absolutely no idea how to help somebody connect with their guides! They are telling me to recap my journey, that would be helpful for people. So here we go.

I began meditating around five years ago. Up to that point I had never been able to meditate. In all of my searching and self help books and YouTube videos every time I would get to the section that they would tell me I needed to meditate, I would skip that section! I feel very strongly that we need to follow our inner guidance, that's what this whole book is about after all! Looking back I realized that it just didn't resonate with me at the time. We need to be ready for things, and it took me some time to be ready to meditate. I realize that some of my aversion to meditation came from my religious background. We were told to never surrender our minds, if you surrendered your mind the devil was gonna take you over and bad things would happen!

I remember years ago going to a class about angels, it was led by a wonderful lady who had a beautiful spirit! She talked about meditation and how we become closer to ourselves with meditation and she had such beautiful, positive energy, that I decided to give it a try. I remember it very vividly. I was laying on my couch meditating and I remembered the energy starting to move in my lower body coming up my legs and starting to feel very weird to me! I immediately panicked and brought myself out of the altered state. I'm not much of a conspiracy theorist, but I do ask myself why does organized religion take such a firm stand against meditation. The answer of course is because it leads to freedom! When you can contact your own higher self, you have guidance for your life. You no longer need the rules and regulations of organized religion.

So, years passed and I didn't meditate. I experienced a winter of many illnesses. I had influenza A, pneumonia, bronchitis... All one right after another! I have asthma as well, so my lungs were a hot mess! I was having lots of trouble breathing, and building my strength back up. So I Googled how to strengthen my lungs and found a breathing technique designed by Wim Hoff. He is a very cool guy! He is in the Guinness Book of world records for the greatest amount of time holding your breath under ice! They call him the iceman you should check him out! He teaches a breathing technique that has you hyper oxygenate, followed by holding your breath, which results in hypoxia. I will let you look this up for yourself, but I can assure you it is a very powerful technique! As I would do the rounds of breathing, in between I would feel very altered. There is no question that the way this breathing affected the chemistry of my body created a very altered state. For lack of a better description, I would say I felt drunk! That swirly feeling that you get when you've had a few drinks. That feeling was enjoyable, so I began to stretch the time between rounds of breathing out, to experience that altered state.

That was so effective for me that I started to research other kinds of meditation. There are many different meditations that are associated with breathing techniques. I remember people saying to me that what I was experiencing wasn't real because anybody would feel strange if they held their breath for too long. I suppose there's some truth to that. But I also think about how Native Americans use different techniques and substances to alter themselves to have spiritual experiences. Many tribes and indigenous peoples do as well. I judged it by how it felt, it felt wonderful! I tried various techniques with a lot of success in feeling altered. I wish I could give justice to what that altered state feels like, but it is very difficult to describe. I would feel energy buzz through my body. I would see things dance behind my eyes. I would see lights; I would see floating clouds that would change shapes and go in and out of my vision. Always with the buzzing hum of energy. At first the energy was less of course, it would start in my hands, or my feet, or sometimes my head. As I practiced meditation the vibration just got more and more intense. I know now that my guides were gently bringing me along. Had I felt too much energy all at one time it would have frightened me, they are always facilitating my success!

Trying to put into words advice to help someone else start this journey is a challenge! I would say to scan your body while you're meditating and see if you find a place that feels different. Just notice it, validate it, your attention is powerful. I remember teaching the breathing technique to a friend and we meditated together and she told me she didn't feel anything. It takes practice and time. The most profound thing that happened during these meditations was when I began to see the night sky. That is the only way I can describe it. I would be in meditation looking behind my eyes at the clouds and the lights moving around and suddenly in the middle there was a little hole, it was very black behind that hole and I could see sparkles of light that looked like stars. The minute I noticed it and got excited, the hole closed and that was it for that day! I had to practice remaining calm when I noticed the opening. It took a lot of time I'm not sure how long, the opening would get bigger and bigger before my excitement would take over and it would then close. Until finally one day I was able to remain calm enough, that the hole completely opened. I was then surrounded by that beautiful night sky. I could literally turn my head from side to side and look into the distance. My eyes would tear because I was enveloped in such a loving sensation. I remember the words coming into my mind that first time, from the 23rd psalm, "and I will dwell in the house of the Lord forever" that is what it felt like. I felt like I was in the presence of God. I didn't see anything that looked like God, just the vastness of space and stars and the sensation of floating and being surrounded by the darkness. So that became the focus of my meditations. Trying to get myself to that point of the sky opening so I could be within that beautiful starry sky. I would feel so many physical sensations during those months and years. I didn't realize the significance of it all so I didn't journal about it or keep track of it in any way.

I had read the book by Joe Dispenza called Becoming Supernatural. It was a very good book that taught me a lot about meditation, I highly recommend it. In the book he shares a lot of scientific evidence that proves the benefits of meditation for the human body and spirit. I would spend time in meditation trying to heal my body. During that time, I was diagnosed with rheumatoid arthritis. I had been having a lot of difficulties with my joints, particularly my feet. After going to the podiatrist and having him tell me there was nothing that he could see the matter with my feet, the doctors all recommended me to a rheumatologist. I was having trouble walking; I was only in my mid 50s so I should not have been so debilitated but I was. I could get around, but I would have days that when I would come home from school and I would sit down on the couch and I can remember thinking I don't care how thirsty I am or how bad I need to go to the bathroom I'm not walking anywhere else...

I have always been a very active person. I've been the queen of diet and exercise over the years. I wasn't able to do anything that required much energy. After they diagnosed me, they put me on some very hard-core medication. It didn't seem to help much. They changed it several times and I ended up with a serious allergic reaction that we later found out had nothing to do with the medication, but at the time, I didn't know that. I stopped all the medication and decided to try a holistic approach. I would do my meditations and I would focus on my body and I would try to focus on the future where my body didn't stop me from doing the things I wanted to do. I am now on a medication that is very effective and I feel great. I believe that the years when this condition developed were affected by my mental state. I know conclusively the mind body connection, there's no doubt in my mind that one affects the other! It is a goal of mine to get off the medication now that I am so happy. I have asked my guides and they basically tell me that taking it or not taking it doesn't really matter. They tell me to make a decision and line up with it!

The reason I mention my physical condition is because it was part of the motivation that kept me meditating. I continued to have lots of physical sensations happened during meditation. The vibrating energy just got more and more intense. I also began to experience tickling on my cheek, and touches on my hands. This never frightened me, which as I write this, is surprising, but it didn't. I guess because I just felt so much love when I meditated and made that connection with the night sky. I think for me having my counselor plant the seed about being an empath validated to me that I was different. It gave me permission to research things of a metaphysical nature. When I happened on to Suzanne Giesemann on YouTube and she validated that everyone has the ability to become a medium, and have a daily relationship with their own guides, it was the permission that I needed to go to the next step. It makes me think about the four-minute mile. For years that was the standard, no one could run faster than a mile in four minutes. But once someone did, lots and lots of people did! I also remember the year that the home run record got broken, it had stood fast for years, but the summer that it got broken, it was broken more than once! For me having someone outside of myself tell me that these things were possible gave me permission to open myself up completely.

I think the easiest thing to try first would be writing. To get into a meditative state and set a notebook on your lap with the intention of bringing through information from your team of guides. It's called automatic writing and you can do some research about that. It wasn't effective for me because I struggled with spelling! I would get writing along and want to write a word that I couldn't spell and it would bring me out of my altered state. So I knew that wasn't going to be the answer for me. As I mentioned earlier when we spoke about the process around your inner child I used my phone as a recording device. My counselor had encouraged me to journal the conversations between myself and my inner child but I had the same problem when it came to spelling. It would disrupt the flow and make the whole process much less effective. But if you are someone who likes to write, journaling can be very effective for people. I am now able to sit down and write information from my guides with no problems but it was not a starting point for me.

I waited five or six weeks after my counselor planted the seed with me before I had the opportunity to try to record my guides. My husband was gone away for the weekend so I knew I would not be disturbed. I laid my phone on my chest and got myself into a meditative state. And I began to pray out loud. I just started to pray, thanking them for being with me, thanking them for guiding and helping me. Then I just started to repeat over and over again, "let the words come". And they did. My guides began to talk using my voice. My voice was altered that first time, it had a bit of an accent. They directed me to try to not listen, to just let the words flow, to step out into that night sky and let the words come. I tried to ask them questions out loud, that was not terribly effective trying to shift back and forth. So they told me to speak the questions in my mind and that they would repeat them so they would be on the recording. They are very helpful lol!

Everyone has a team of guides. We are born with them. It is my understanding that we have several, but maybe it's only one that is with us our entire life. The rest of the team is dynamic, it changes with the needs of the individual. That is very cool if you think about it, we have unlimited access to all kinds of experts! We have an internal internet! The challenge is learning to access it, and learning to trust it. Many people are able to get signs to validate what their guides tell them. For example, a message comes through in meditation and you ask your guides to give you a sign that will validate it was them and not your imagination. You clear your mind and they will drop something in, it could be anything. Let's say they drop in a red bird. Within the next few days, you will see the red bird. When that happens, I think it's very important that you thank your team and validate that indeed, you had trustworthy communication, and you build on that.

It didn't work like that for me. I received very few signs throughout my development. I received lots of physical sensations and manifestations within my body that reinforced to me that I was indeed interacting with something different. I haven't found on YouTube anyone whose development was like mine! I think signs are a very common way, and easy way, for our guides to interact with us it just was not part of my journey. I came into this experience with a great deal of faith in God. I believe that my journey has been around developing my faith to an even greater level. But practice using the sign method, because I think that is the most common and easy path. I think it's helpful for people to write down when they ask for the sign, so they can go back and look to see how many they get. Remember your left brain, your ego self will try to get involved and probably will from time to time. When you do not get the sign you were looking for, just let that flow by and know that next time you probably will get it. I do believe a certain amount of faith is required in this work. Perhaps the word belief is better, but for me it's been faith. Let's ask my team if they have anything they would like to say about connecting with your guides...

You are asking us to help you facilitate your readers in being able to access their team of non-physical helpers. You are frustrated that your description might not be that helpful. The reality is, it does not take that much help. The individual needs to be within the vibrational range of this contact for it to happen. As they work doing the processes that are within this book and they are consciously and intentionally working to raise their vibration they are getting closer and closer to the ability to be able to make contact, for themselves, with their higher self. Be reminded dear ones, that we have no concept of time, there is absolutely no sense of impatient on our side of the veil, as we watch you throughout your life. We interact with you in many ways, the nudges and the intuition that you develop throughout your lifetime is us dear ones. That "feeling" that you get, to go this way, or that, that is us. To intentionally practice this process, to ask for help going right or left and taking just a moment and listening... Asking yourself how did it feel when you made the decision to go right, and then what were the results. This is a good way to begin. First acknowledging that you know we are there. Spending time in your daily meditations, asking us to interact with you, asking for the touch on your cheek, asking for the vibration in your hands. Asking and then waiting with anticipation, knowing that it will come, if not today, it will come. Having belief and faith that you are on the road to this ability. Having a knowing that we are celebrating every step you take along that path. It is important to remember dear ones, that this is a dimension of free will. When you intentionally decide to utilize your guidance from non-physical it opens the door so to speak. Set that intention, often throughout your day, bringing your consciousness into your mind for a moment, feel the blending that will happen and know we are right there listening.

You are asking if your consciousness and your guides are the same thing. We would remind you that we are all one Kelly, we are all energy, we are all vibration. Consciousness is a part, an extension of your higher self, that is experiencing life through this vessel that you call your body. We are one with your higher self. Learning to distinguish between your consciousness and your physical vessel, seeing them as two entirely different entities, is a powerful thing. It is your consciousness, as you shift it and move it away from the ego mind, that can interact with us. You are not tied to this vessel, that shifting, moving away from your human mind, is what you are practicing when you are practicing meditation. There are many tips, tricks, and techniques that help various humans identify their consciousness and learn to control its perspective. The consciousness enjoys and has chosen to come experience life through the vessel known as Kelly. The consciousness rejoices however in the ability to move away with intention and blend with those on the other side of the veil. Do not think dear ones that your consciousness wants to be away from the vessel for you chose to express yourself in this way. It is the road to enlightenment, as you identify the power that you have, moving your consciousness away from the ego mind, to quiet it so that you can clearly blend with those who are non-physical.

We are asking you now Kelly, to take note where your consciousness is as we speak through you. Feel your body sitting on this couch, feel the computer in your lap, you are even able to insert punctuation as we speak. Where is your perspective? "I feel like it's out on the right-hand side up a bit." *That is right. When we first asked you, you confused your right and left in your altered state and wondered why we would be on the left side. When we say we, we mean your consciousness blended with us. When you focused, you realized we are always on your right, putting the distance of the right side of your brain between us and the left brain, ego mind. It may be, for some, the left-hand side will feel more natural, it does not matter. Being outside of the human vessel is the part you strive for.*

You are asking if there is any more we would like to say. We would just point out that we are also the voice within your head, within your heart. It is difficult for the human to identify our voice because it is so close to what you would call your thoughts. It has been there since you were born. The challenge is identifying it within the din of confusion that most human minds dwell. Again this is the reason why we encourage meditation, it is a practicing of quieting the mind. When the mind is quiet our voice can be heard. We will remind the reader that this one is still practicing clear communication with us within her head. She enjoys the validation of the shivering in her jaw that she is experiencing right now as we speak through her. But she is learning, she is practicing, that is all we would ask. We would remind Kelly now to speak of some of those early times when she was at school that she practiced her interactions with us.

They dropped into my mind a memory of last winter. I would do my meditations in the morning, this was before I began to channel them, and I would set my intention to interact with them throughout the day. If I had a decision to make, even a small one I would try to remember to ask them. I would ask them yes or no. I would say is the answer yes, and I would wait and see how my body felt. I would say is the answer no and do the same thing. I did make progress in feeling the slight sensations that would go up the back of my neck or down my back, basically anywhere within my body I might feel goose pimples or a little wave of energy. This was a great way to practice the connection.

I am thinking about what they said about it becoming easier as we raise our vibration using the methods they have given us throughout this book. Then I thought I didn't have those methods prior to blending with them. I was just meditating. What I realize is, when I began doing counseling and doing the inner child work, I was raising my vibration as I let go of those influences from the past. I realized that the internal dialogue that is set up in childhood, that follows us throughout our lives, until we heal it, brings our vibration down. I imagine the path is different for everyone. I think that is why they are leading me to lay out things in this book the way I am. For some I imagine healing the inner child would have to happen before their vibration could raise enough to blend with their guides. For others perhaps just doing the techniques to raise your vibration daily would be enough. I'm not really sure. I only know what worked for me.

Chapter Thirteen

Mother Earth

I have never considered myself to be much of a champion when it comes to the earth. I have learned a lot of different things over the years. I remember learning about the way cattle are raised for human consumption, how inhumane it is and being very uncomfortable with the thought, but not compelled to change what I ate in response to that. I'm a bit embarrassed to admit that, but it's the truth. I've never been very good at recycling, and I have laid in a supply of straws that will last me the rest of my life because I hate paper straws and I have sensitive teeth, so I like to drink out of a straw. These are just several things that describe my relationship with the earth. Not that I have not always appreciated the earth throughout my life because I have. To revel in the beauty of a sunset or looking out at my lake fills my heart with love and awe.

Years ago, I had a lady read me, I was not sure what that meant but I remember her telling me at the time that she used the vision of a rose to tell her information about the person she was reading. She saw my rose as lush and full and open at the top but only a single stem down to the earth. What that represented to her, she explained, was that I was not particularly grounded to the earth. I understood that to a point at the time, but not completely. I was always connected to the higher realm. I could feel my connection to God and Jesus and the angels very clearly throughout my life, but I didn't feel any connection to Mother Earth. Until one day during meditation she reached her heart up and enveloped me and we had a conversation. Even as I write this, I know how incredible it sounds. As with all things, test it in your heart. She knew I needed to develop my relationship with her to evolve to the next level in my development. And she wanted to help me...

It began like any other meditation; I was channeling my guides when all of a sudden, my voice got deeper. I am going to interject throughout the transcription to try to make sense of it for both of us. I will title those as narrations because there is a lot of back-and-forth conversation during this. That way you will know the part that came through during the transmission and the narrations that I'm adding now. The following is some of what happened...

Send your energy down, we are trying to blend with you. There is a message from Mother Earth, feeling our presence, feeling the energy of our words. You step into that space and allow us to talk to you. You are so very loved and supported on this earth. (The words were coming very slow and my voice was a bit deeper than usual) *Feel the difference in the energy, send your roots to my heart and I will hold them. The rocks and the soil hold your energy Kelly. Pulling you to your higher self, supporting you in your journey. Feel the love that the earth has for you, feeling the support and the safety that I have for you. You ask if I am but one. I am the elements, the power of the elements, the energy of the elements resides in myself and my atmosphere. Do not let the oddness of your voice distract you, step away from that and allow us to speak through you. We know it is difficult. You'll feel the difference in your energy as we come through. It is very important for your evolution on the path that you are traveling, the path that you have been on since birth. You feel like it is a detriment that this awakening has happened within you at what you consider to be your advanced years. There is no time Kelly, age does not exist. You have been traveling this path for eternity...*

Narration- I have wondered why this journey of awakening has happened at this stage in life. I am now 60, not old but not a spring chicken either. There is a part of me that feels guilty that I didn't catch on quicker. I think it's part of my journey of surrender and acceptance to acknowledge that things happen in their own time. We cannot dictate what we think is the best plan. Source knows the perfect timing for our highest good.

You are anxious for our message, which is good, you want to know what we have for you and your growth because you are excited for your growth and passionate for your growth and you know that is the path that you are to be on. Awareness of the relationship between Mother Earth and the collective is an important piece of the puzzle. Knowing every blade of grass, every tree, and every leaf, and every drop of rain contains within it the energy of the universe. You can connect to that energy and it will serve you, keeping you safe, truly grounded. Now you have an understanding of the world and what it truly means to Be. *So that when you travel through the many expanses of the universe, when you step into the other dimensions, it is us that will call you back* (at this point my voice is getting difficult to understand, I am flexing and moving and straining because the energy is so different than what I'm used to and the message is so far from my level of current understanding) *We couldn't let it happen until you developed this with us in order for this next level to unfold.*

Narration-they are speaking of the fear that I have around completely surrendering into my meditations. I have read about others who are able to move between dimensions. In a very intentional way bringing back information and various things. My meditations get very deep but there is a point when I feel like I'm pulling back because I am scared. So much of my understanding of reality has changed, my mind has certainly opened up to infinite possibilities. I can't help but wonder if one of those possibilities would be for me to just raise my vibration so high that I don't come back to my body. I'm embarrassed to put that into words, but it is the truth. I love my life! I love my husband and my family and I want to live out this time on earth. My rational mind acknowledges that it doesn't make any sense for everything that I've learned and everything that I've gone through in the past year to have happened just for me to disappear from this reality. I also think that my level of connection or lack thereof to the earth plays a big part in this. This melding of energy between myself and Mother Earth is life changing, it has brought me to a whole new level of understanding, both physical and energetic understanding.

It is a safety net, the net that is the Gaia energy from above in the clouds in our entire atmosphere we are a living being and you are part of us. You are one of our cells that we have called forth and yet the whole of us, you melded with us, we are a cell of a larger creative force. That is also a cell in a larger creative force and it goes on and on forever, for eternity.

Narration-this is so far beyond my understanding that I'm tempted to leave it out of the book. They are urging me to include it so I will. I have no idea what it means, I understand the principle but I've never heard anything like this before. Perhaps it it's a metaphor and we will figure that out later on but for now I must say my mind is officially blown!

It is the piece that has been missing Kelly, you are feeling like something is falling into place and it is, you needed your connection strengthened. You've always had a connection but it was not the intimate, personal relationship that it will be now. That was the next layer that needed to happen in your evolution. You are asking what we would have you do. Develop that relationship as you have developed your relationship with that which is not us. You know that it is all one, the frequencies you have played with and experienced, the frequencies of one end of the spectrum so to speak, that is a good way of understanding this, we represent the spectrum that goes to the center of Mother Earth. We represent the strength and the solidity, the power of this planet as it supports you in this incarnation. Your path is not to be, (laughing) *the tree hugger,* (my voice is shivering violently) *it doesn't mean that all of a sudden you have to worry about every piece of trash that is generated, that is not your path. Your path is the energy, to experience the energy fluctuations that you can feel when you are in the rain. The energy that you can feel when your feet are bare on the planet, on the earth, what does it feel like? What is the difference between standing on a rock and standing on the sand with your feet in the ocean? It connects you; one drop of water connects you to the element of water, the power of water. One flame connects you to all the flames that have ever been or ever will be, the power of fire. You're laughing and saying that you've never really liked wind. The energy of wind has been uncomfortable for you because you are not in tune to it. That is an area of growth, the power of wind carries the energy around your planet blending it all. You just were not in touch enough with your own energy, to be able to enjoy the beautiful power of the wind, but you will now. What does fire have to say to you? There is knowing in all of it, the beautiful rock that you have always loved, the feeling of sand beneath your feet, the increasing of your connection to Mother Earth, to us.*

Narration-I have never considered myself to be particularly connected to the earth but she is explaining to me that I have been. I have rocks in every room in my house practically. I have collected rocks since I was just a little girl. They've always been very precious to me. This was something I shared with my mother, when she passed away the very first thing that I wanted from her house was her bowl of rocks, that was what meant the most to me. And the rain, I have always been drawn to the rain. Even as an adult I would put my bathing suit on and go out and play in the rain. I love to swim in the rain and watch the drops bounce off my beautiful lake. It's so strange when I think about it, I have always wanted to be on the water. I have a beautiful home with a lovely lawn, and beach out front. But I want to be on my boat just floating out in the middle. It's actually a bone of contention sometimes between Michael and I because he just wants to relax on the beach but I want to be out on my boat! Now I realize it is because when we are touching the water, we are connected to the expanse that the water is touching Mother Earth and it feels comforting to us. As she is explaining her elements, it makes me wonder if there is some kind of usable power for the human in their connection to the elements. I do not know...

The upsets of your body have been a result of the lack of conscious connection, conscious connection to Mother Earth and her elements. Using the connections consciously as you move forward. Light that comes forth from the sun, from the stars, from the moon, is also one of our components. (I'm seeing the galaxies all connected with a line of energy coming to earth, part of the collective, part of the connection.)

You're asking what we want you to know. It is an awareness Kelly. An awareness of the oneness, the co-creative interwoven capacity that you can consciously utilize. The connection to Mother Earth and the fact that when you are connected to Mother Earth and we are connected to everything else, it strengthens your power. Up to this point you have been like a pebble on the beach. You've been radiating up to the collective with great power, great energy certainly from the perspective that you've had up to this time. But when you come from the space of being connected and held in safety and comfort by your Mother Earth, by Gaia, you can step forward into the other dimensions, into your evolution. Do not feel the need to put a name to it Kelly, you are doing so well at allowing the unfolding. There is no end, there's no end to the game of this, it is a journey, this is a journey. (Yes, knowing that this is it exactly, this place of knowingness that I have been understanding, that you've allowed me to understand, helps me to understand this (I am crying) they are showing me in my mind the earth and the earth's atmosphere.)

For lack of better understanding for this moment in time, if we were to consider the earth as an individual, we would consider the planet itself with everything that is upon the physical surface and we would also consider the atmosphere to be the outermost actual surface of the beingness that is Mother Earth. This is a good way to think about it Kelly, you will understand it to a greater degree at a different time. For now, this is the best way to think about it. You are not <u>upon</u> Mother Earth, you are <u>within</u> her. She holds you; she surrounds you; she uses all of her abilities and the elements to support the life that she brings forth. It is overwhelming to think about the beingness that is Mother Earth. When you think of her as a being. (I'm crying hard), (feeling the beingness of Mother Earth, the beingness, and that there are many like her and that she is our mother (sobbing now) feeling the love that she has for each of us within her as she gets ready to birth us to our next level. Sobbing... Seeing the beingness of Mother Earth and knowing that she is but a cell in another being that is greater than her (in my mind and consciousness I am seeing a massive expansion from her being but one cell, but that we are her children, we are contained within her. Until I had this knowing, I would not be able to draw forward in whatever way it's supposed to be that I don't understand right now. How do I not feel the pain, knowing the things that are happening on you if I see you as a loving being and the things that mankind are doing to you do you how do I not feel the sorrow?)

Narration-at this point I am incredibly altered. I am sobbing, my jaw is shivering, my body is flexing and moving. As I reread this, I see that they are shifting perspectives, I believe at this time my team came in and started to talk to me to help me understand. It's very difficult for me to explain this but at this point I was so blended with Mother Earth that I felt her pain and her sorrow. More accurately I felt my human perspective of her pain and sorrow. I was writhing with it, completely overwhelmed, gasping for breaths between sobs, it was very difficult to understand the recording.

Let the voice come calmly, let the voice come, I don't want you to feel that pain my daughter, experiencing the contrast, just allow the voice to come through. This is a good way for you to understand it. It does not hurt us anymore than your skin tears and bruises hurt, yes there are varying degrees of pain that are caused by these wounds, for lack of a better way of saying it, but that is part of our evolution. Do not feel that pain Kelly, it is not part of your journey. Allow us to feel our pain, you feel your physical pain. That is a very good analogy, it is not exactly correct, but it serves the purpose for now. Take away the sorrow that you feel, because in the same way that you are learning to embrace and live in joy while seeing hardships that are around you, we embrace, and experience joy while observing the hardships that are around us. We know that it is the ultimate expansion of who we are as Mother Earth. The knowledge that you now have access to, the knowledge of how things of the other realm, the esoteric realm, interacts with our children, our cells. The place of coming together with the knowingness that is us, Mother Earth.

Narration-this knowing that they are talking about right here is the ultimate purpose of this book. It is a space of understanding. It is that moment in time when you know that you are standing at the brink of infinite possibilities. It is that faith, that knowing that you are completely and totally loved and supported. It is the present moment. It holds all power and all possibilities. As I write these words I am vibrating from head to toe, they so want for humanity to be able to understand the power that is at their fingertips. They are describing us as not being together with Mother Earth, not walking upon Mother Earth, but that we are a cell that make up Mother Earth. As they speak of the esoteric realm that interacts with us, they are describing that point of blending, of merging, that happens between the energy of consciousness and the energy of Mother Earth, remembering, of course, that all is one.

You feel the living, breathing, entity that we are. You know that you are held within us and loved by us and supported by us with everything that has gone before in this evolutionary time. All the knowing, all the knowledge, is kept within the blades of grass, within the drops of water. You do not need to feel sorrow for the blade of grass getting cut by your lawn mower as those blades of grass have chosen their place on this planet and what they absorb, as an entity in this particular space, but connected to the whole. What you are moving towards, is being connected to the whole. Not yet understanding what the whole is. We bring forth this knowledge of Mother Earth and the knowings from past experiences of those like you, that knowing is kept in the very fabric that is us. It can be accessed through us. With your knowing and intention as you honor and love us and connect your heart to ours. Feel the love and the connection bringing joy Kelly not sorrow. (Crying again) *you will figure out that this is a huge piece of information and a huge blending of energy as you blend with us.* (My jaw is shaking dramatically and I am crying.) *Those tears are not sorrow, your physical body has joined with us and is experiencing these things as we pour our energy into your physical being, into your cells, as you say yes and you invite us in, there is a blending. As we blend for the knowing, the knowing that all is well. Everything is living out its purpose. Do not see any of it with judgment, you are seeing the pictures of the cattle being killed in an unkind way and all of the things that could wrap up your human emotional self if it was allowed to do so. As it has with many whose evolution started with the connection to us. They have not reached out to the knowing quite yet but they are on exactly the right path.*

Narration-as this was coming through, they were giving me a knowing that all creatures, all components of Mother Earth come forth with choice. That the cattle had some level of understanding that they would be sacrificing themselves to feed people and chose to come to earth anyway. This isn't exactly correct but the essence of what they want us to understand is there. They are teaching us to live in the present moment without judgment. When we sit in judgment of what we consider to be an injustice or something that is morally wrong we are still sitting in the energy of judgment. Anytime we do that we are losing our connection to our power.

We are showing you a beam from the center of us to all that is and back. That beam goes and comes and goes and comes and goes farther each time, and deeper each time. Do not think of Mother Earth as a single entity, she is but a cell. (They explained to me a continuum of frequencies and that I had been mostly on one end of the continuum. The continuum is reaching out into a beingness that I can call consciousness on this side and they're explaining that they are part of a consciousness that is on the other end and that Mother Earth is but a cell and that it is all one. It is all creation and creation is full of frequencies and access to the frequencies requires connection.) *You are tipping your toe, so to speak into the knowledge of the vastness of the frequencies that you have, up to this point, not had access to. We are showing you the little Wi-Fi icon again to help you have an understanding. Let's just say to the left and to the right, on the right-hand side you have grown and grown and expanded and come to many layers of knowing. You got to a place where if you're left-hand side did not expand it was holding you back. Now you are on the left-hand side even in your readings your left and right feel different, your right-hand side feels stronger, this is a very good analogy so you now have an understanding.*

You know that there is a relationship that you are going to begin with the energy that is Gaia, that is Mother Earth. You are going to begin that relationship, that back and forth asking for insights in this moment. Feeling it on the left side just as a way of understanding and it is a perfect way to understand it for you right now, just go with this understanding. There are limitless frequencies on the side that is Gaia, connected to the All that is on this side of the frequencies that go forever. But they are all one. (They just showed me that on this left side, creating its own Wi-Fi icon, are expanding layers and layers of frequencies that are growing and evolving in that direction and it is it's own layer of frequencies.) *There are others that will complete the one complete whole circle. There are many lines going in many directions with the layers all radiating out to create the entire circle. That is a good description, you had a flat description in your mind now make it 3D going out in all of those directions, with the knowings that can happen in all of those directions and that is all very true and powerful. Don't think of Gaia as different, it's just a different frequency, think of the television and all the different channels you're tuning into, different channels that have different gifts and different knowings, different abilities. The feeling that you have, that you need these frequencies for the whole to expand is correct. Bring this into your day as a human, as a child of Gaia, as a cell within Gaia, as a being within Gaia, connected, one with the whole of Gaia, and one with the whole of creation, supported by the all, surrounded by the all. The consciousness is what knows that we are what we are as you walk forth with that awareness and you feel the air on your face you know that is you in your mother's womb being held in safety and yes that has the potential of giving you the security that you need to perhaps step out and travel between, you hesitate to say the word, dimensions, because it seems a tad lacking with this new understanding. Frequency/dimension they are human words but they help you to understand and it serves you well within the knowing, you are to find joy.*

Rejoice in the blade of grass that gets cut, knowing that it is fulfilling its purpose. Rejoice in the animal that has chosen to come forward into that environment, they are serving a purpose. You are struggling with that; we are saying there is no sorrow in that Kelly, you can rejoice because there is no judgment. Do you feel hurt or slayed to your core when you get a cut? Of course you do not, a cut heals, it regenerates, it becomes new, that is exactly how it works on us. There is growth happening for many beings, many paths, all correct, all perfect and beautiful, rejoice in them all. You should not have any kind of sorrow for any person with any belief that seems extreme, for they are exactly like the blade of grass as it gets cut off. Because the soul, that is that person, will be fine, just as the blade of grass will be fine. The energy that can come up into your body from Mother Earth, your body as it is connected to Mother Earth will act like an antenna or beacon, it will draw you back, there is no fear,

As I have transcribed this download it has been incredibly emotional. There are so many huge concepts within it, it's difficult to know where to even begin. But when you think about being held within your mother, in total and complete safety and being reminded of that when you feel the wind on your face, or even the ground beneath your feet, what comfort there is in that. Showing us the infinite number of creative frequencies that are available to us, emanating out from Mother Earth, blending with the creative energy of the cosmos, traveling in and out, this is that pathway that they want us to utilize for creation.

Addendum-I received this download from Mother Earth in October 2022 and was guided to include it in this book. At the time there were parts of it that were very confusing to me. As I transcribed this download into my book I was still confused. I did my best to transcribe it in a way that would be understandable. When I receive downloads they give me many forms of communication. Pictures and knowings that help me to understand what they are bringing through. I have finished my book now, and I have gone back to the beginning for the editing process. What I realized is that the information that is in this chapter is the foundation for what will come later. Remember this chapter when you read the second part of this book, the Angel section. The angels will bring through understanding. Try to envision the three dimensional model of the energy flowing in all directions through Mother Earth, out to the cosmos and back, that Mother Earth described. You will understand more later...

Chapter Fourteen

Being Overwhelmed

After my first book became available to the public, I was contacted by a lovely woman who I have known for years. We didn't spend much time together but we were always pleasant in passing. She read my book and reached out to me on Facebook to tell me what an impact it was having on her. She has experienced many of the same kinds of energetic happenings and wanted to get together to discuss it. I was thrilled at the thought of someone being impacted by my work so I happily accepted her invitation to meet for lunch. We had a wonderful conversation; I had known that she was a Reiki master and that she did sessions in her home. I was very interested to hear about her spiritual journey. We decided to take it to the next level and meet at her house and trade energetic gifts. I was going to receive a Reiki session and then I was going to give her a channeled reading or a mediumship reading or both!

We very much enjoyed the experience, both of us gained a great deal from spending time together, so we decided to meet again the next week. The following is a transcript of the conversation between her and my team. We started the session by asking for whoever had a message for our highest good to come through. This is part of the conversation. I felt that much of it was so pertinent to the average person on their journey that it would be helpful.

Debbie, "can you tell me about the akashic records"

Kelly, "I am a blank slate about the akashic records this will be very interesting to see what we get" (laughing)

You struggle Kelly, because you want to have input on the answers as they come through or at least you think you do. But we have told you time and again that the answers come from us. So let us speak of the akashic records. Let us speak of that place, that vibrational holding tank, so to speak, that holds within it all of the experiences, that's not quite right, all of the frequencies, the vibrational signature of all that has ever been or ever will be. Remind yourself of the concept of time, and that the only time is now. Everything that has ever been is now, everything that is ever going to be, is now. It is very difficult for the human to grasp that concept, but you ladies have a beginning understanding of that. So, when you take that understanding of time, the akashic records is the vibrational place, place isn't exactly right, this is a concept that is very difficult for your language to understand and express. But for lack of a better word let's go with place. It is a holding place for the what has been and the what will be. Do you have a specific question about the akashic records?

Debbie,"I just wondered if it would be worth it for me to explore and maybe have a session, or is it not necessary?"

What we would say to you dear one, is what we have said to this one, let us speak directly to your feelings of being overwhelmed. The esoteric world of energy and understandings is vast. It is all correct, we want to restate or validate that as well, there is no wrong path in any of this. Knowing that is a powerful part of being. We would ask for you to sit with it and perhaps a focusing down, perhaps a "one thing at a time" kind of mentality would serve you best at this time. We would say the people, who do the work with the akashic records, are on a correct, and blessed journey, just as you and Kelly are, absolutely all of the paths are valid dear ones. There are so many, many paths and if you strew your energy between them all, your energy will not have time to grow the way that your heart and soul wants it to grow.

Debbie, "I find myself trying to get bits and pieces from all the paths and putting them together."

It's a very confusing puzzle. Not all of the pieces will fit. That does not make them wrong because they don't fit together. Because they don't fit together does not make it incorrect. The pieces within your path will fit together, not every piece, of every path, is meant to fit into yours. We would ask you to consider the feelings that you have experienced lately of being out of balance, or overwhelmed, we would even describe it as scattered. We have sensed those feelings from you in this recent time. You have opened the door to a knowing and a welcoming around your spiritual growth. Do not look outside of yourself dear one, sit with those internal knowings, they will lead you. In just the joining of the two of you, you both have varying gifts and tools of awakening that are different, but they feel like they fit, do they not? We would say this is enough for now. Explore this, you have both have had experiences in your lives when things would run their course. That may be what will happen with this as well in time. You will both know, continue as long as you are both feeling the blessing in the coming together. It may take multiple lifetimes before you have run the course of this relationship.

This one asks us often to recap, because it is hard for her human mind to grasp the entire idea. What we are saying is this, their requires, but requires isn't exactly right because you know there is no wrong and we do not want to get you on the path of filling your heads full of should and shouldn'ts, that's not where we want you to be at all. But there is benefit to focus. Imagine if you would a garden, you plant a small patch over here,(they point to a spot on the floor close to me) *with some specific seeds. But you spend all of your time watering over here and over there and over here*(they point away in many directions). *This will grow,*(pointing to the first spot) *there will be growth because that is the nature of the seeds and as they come together with the soil and the light, in spite of you. But with your specific intention and attention with your watering hose and gentle care of pruning and weeding and care that can be given to this small patch, this small patch can grow to be a miraculous thing! This is the truth in spiritual development. The thing that resonates with you is the thing, it is not wrong for you to tip your toe into various pools or check the soil in the different spots, this is not what we are saying, there is no wrong to this at all. Check the spot find the spot that feels just right, put your seeds there and tend them, put your water, we feel that that is a very good analogy.*

Debbie, "So basically, they are saying to focus on what I know, not have as much focus on all the other things I've been thinking about, maybe those will come in time? Or I will get a message that it's time maybe to set my intention to do more?"

You have for some time felt a yearning have you not? A yearning for something more,

Debbie, "yes"

We do not mean to say the growth does not come from that feeling of seeking. We do not mean to say that you are not still seeking. Let's go back to the present moment, you cannot fill your present moment with ten things and expect any of them to do well. So we would say to you, you are doing very well with your Reiki business. It is serving you in multiple ways. You shared with this one that you have plenty of business and you feel good about the fact that you are indeed a Reiki master. You are doing good work with your practice. That no longer needs the watering and the pruning that it did at one time. At one time it required a great deal from you, did it not. But it doesn't any longer, it is second nature to you. That is wonderful, that is that flower box that comes back year after year and needs very little tending because it has the plants that know what to do and grow by themselves. You are looking for a direction Debbie, your heart, your spiritual heart is striving. We would say that that is a good thing. We feel that you are on the edge of the next leveling up, so to speak.

When you began the Reiki, there was a period of self development at that time was there not?

Debbie, "Somewhat, I didn't know where to turn and I turned to Reiki."

That was exactly what we wanted you to remember, you were searching and you found the Reiki and the Reiki served this wonderful purpose and continues to. We are not saying yes or no, to go this way or that way. We always say to this one when she gets confused, go back to basics, this is what we are saying to you. The human condition is like a spiral, you are going and going and going, but then there might be some steps that you might struggle with a bit and then it is gradual and it goes and goes and then oops there's some more steps that you must struggle across.

What you are feeling right now are those steps Debbie, it's not that you are a long way off your path, it is just a little bit of a change that is in the ether, that you are dancing with, that you are wanting. So we would just ask you, to ask yourself, which thing resonates with you the most. But remember it comes from that place of personal growth. You spent some wonderfully reflective time with your journal looking deep, those things do need attention. As we have used the example of the spiral, as one grows the tightness and the stuckness that can be down here at the bottom needs to be healed in order for the top to get the momentum that it will get.(They were moving my hands demonstrating a small funnel shaped spiral that got larger and larger as it got to the top). So the journey of awakening is a journey of self growth. You confuse yourself sometimes when you get too focused on what can help and serve others, when you need to be doing the work to help and serve yourself. Then trusting that if there is an alternate plan for you, in how you spend your days so to speak, it will come.

Debbie and I went on to have a wonderful conversation around personal growth. This concept of inner child continues to bring itself to the forefront in so many ways. Those synchronicities make me know how important the work around the inner child is. Debbie had been using her journal to dive deep within herself to unravel the reasons that she might feel stuck. We both felt blessed to know that we are learning tools to help us with this process. We acknowledged that this inner child, inner critic work will likely never be over. I believe that we will heal to a level that then opens us to be able to grow. Then we will discover the next level that needs to be healed for more growth, and so on.

I feel like this message that came through in mine and Debbie's conversation was very important. Since I have started this journey, it has been a constant battle to not get sucked down different rabbit holes. They have said time and again that all paths are correct. That means that if you are living a life as a Jehovah witness and that is how you believe and that is what is in your heart that path is completely correct for you. That is true for any religion, any spiritual practice. All of these different paths have gifts and processes and practices that can use up one's time. We have to be very discerning as we develop because if we are not none of our gifts will grow to fruition.

Even in the process of writing these books, I have to remind myself that I still must tend to my own spiritual growth. What that means for me is, I need time to meditate often. Not just connecting to my team for conversations and information. Even as I write this I find it amazing. The meditations that are just quiet, when you let your energy soar, are rejuvenating. We need that time for our energy to reboot. They are showing me in my mind right now, the minister who selflessly works day and night tending to his flock, but forgets to tend to his own soul, his own spirituality. That weakens the individual and makes it much easier to step off the path. They bring me back to the present moment, reminding me that a simple breath filled with love and knowing, and connection feeds the soul. But we must stop long enough to take the breath.

As I wrote that my jaw began to shiver so I know they have something they want to say...

You have touched upon a concept of strength versus weakness. This is an important part of your work. Moving forward living a human life is difficult. Living a human life in these times of being bombarded with information and ideas from outside of oneself is full of pitfalls and obstacles. As we move forward, we will discuss ways to strengthen one's resolve. Strengthening ones focused as they develop the ability to shift their consciousness to that higher state of being with more consistency and stability.

Chapter Fifteen

Path to Joy

I decided one day to overcome my fear and do a live event online. I had already purchased a zoom account so there's no limit on how long the meeting can go but I hadn't used it yet. To be honest I had some fear around the issue. I realized that I have been a teacher and I have spoken in front of people for years, but for some reason this felt different. One morning I made-up my mind to do it, just do it! I very quickly set the time and the date and I needed to give it a title. I thought what are people most concerned with right now, it is just a few weeks before Christmas, and I thought joy. The path to joy, everyone is working on that! I titled my presentation <u>The Path to Joy</u> and posted it to my Facebook page. I then leaned back in meditation to ask what I should talk about, what did they have to say about joy. The following is our conversation.

There is no path to joy, it is not a path, that is why humans find it so hard to find. Because joy is the present moment, there is no journey between you and it, it is the present moment.(Doesn't that figure! After I already titled my presentation, and sent an invitation out on Facebook!) *All things will lead you to the present moment, because the present moment is all you have. When the human speaks about the path to joy, they have immediately set themselves up for struggle, set themselves up for difficulties, because they are having a "what am I going to do to get myself there" mentality. That is not what you want to perpetuate, that is just not the way to go about it, and that's why humans struggle.*

When you are in the present moment, welcome joy, say hello to joy, you are welcome here, come on in. You are beckoning it to you, you are not moving towards it. It is a fundamental error that humans have made for a very long time around the things that they want. They feel like even when they apply the principles of the law of attraction, they are moving themselves down a path, so to speak, to whatever it is that they want to be a vibrational match to. When in fact the timeline collapses before you and brings the next present moment into your experience.

You are not going to create joy, joy just is. Do you create love? Do you create sadness? Do you create humor? It is an incorrect idea that humans create emotions. Emotions are a judgment. You see something happen and from your human perspective you judge it as good and you allow yourself to feel happy. You see something that you judge as bad and you allow yourself to feel sad or guilty. The emotional response is a result of the duality of your world. To have an understanding of this, to even begin to entertain the idea of it, in your mind, is a huge step forward in your evolution. It all boils down to perspective. We have said this to you many times, two people experiencing the exact same thing can have entirely different experiences. Humans are at the mercy of their emotions; we want to plant the seed that it doesn't have to be that way. You are saying that this is convoluted, actually it is incredibly simple.

You are asking, if joy just is, why don't we experience joy all the time. That is because of your vibrational frequency, your vibrational signature of the present moment, you are making a choice and you're not choosing joy. It is not outside of you Kelly, it is within. The words that one uses around this topic are very important. It is not a calling to you, it is an embracing of it, it is already right there. It is already right there. All the human needs to do is to just say hello and acknowledge that it's there and wrap your arms around it and squeeze it to you tight and know that it is the present moment, the present moment is joy.

You want a few more details around the workings of your mind around this because it is a fairly new concept for you to grasp. You, in your thinking mind say to yourself, I want to be more joyful. Even in that statement there is an inherent flaw. When you put the energy of <u>want</u> in it, it is proclaiming to the universe that you don't have it. It is the energetic match for the <u>lack</u> of whatever it is that you want. State to the universe "I am joy" and even as you state that you say, I don't <u>feel</u> joy, why would I say that I <u>am</u> joy. We understand that, how about if you were to say,"Joy lives within me, joy is within me, joy is accessible to me all the time, joy is my constant companion, joy is who I am, joy is my right, joy is my position, joy is my understanding." When you say those words, you can feel the change in your vibration can you not? (YES!)

We have said many times as have others like us, the purpose of life is joy. If joy resides always within you, then aren't we also saying that the purpose of life, is <u>you</u>? Think about what we are saying Kelly, the purpose of life is you. <u>You</u> are the purpose of life; you are the purpose of this existence. You have come into this existence with many tools, with many different sets of rules for the game so to speak. But a misunderstanding that humans have is that they feel that they are seeking something that is outside of them, when it all resides within.

Let's go to the concept of time once again, the present moment is all that there is. The present moment is the only thing that humans have and can set claim to. Only the present moment, there are no worries about what can happen next, there are no concerns about what happened yesterday, that is the power, my dear girl. When you can sit in that present moment without any thought for tomorrow and without any judgment about yesterday, the present moment is now, it's right now, for your enjoyment. Nothing can add to or take away from what is within the human, you think it can, you give many, many things power in your creative experience, but there is no external influence that has any power, the only influence is the power that you, within your internal vibration stance, create.

So, we say to you, let's think about the toolbox that goes into that creative ability. Imagination is a wonderful tool in your toolbox. To just fantasize, to just go into your mind if something is happening around you that isn't pleasing, go into your mind and make it different. We are dropping into your head the old technique of picturing everyone in the audience in their underwear. Think about what that actually is. It is utilizing the present moment in a fantastical kind of way to create something that is going to rise your vibration because wouldn't it be funny if everyone were sitting in their underwear? That has been a tool that has been available to humans for a long time. But you don't see the strength and value and the power in these simple tools, you want it to be difficult. You are human and you feel like the road needs to be difficult. The reason why you resonated so completely with the Abraham information was because the very first thing that you listened to said, take your hands off the oars and go with the flow of the river, and that resonated so completely with you and it is so powerful and so true. There is nothing for the human to do to be joyful. They just need to be joyful. Use the tool of your imagination, picture the dancing monkeys, picture the giggling grandchild, whatever it takes for you to picture, in that moment, to raise your vibrational output.

You are asking what if you are in the midst of sorrow or in the midst of trauma or drama. We know that is difficult for you because you are giving the experience a judgment. You are judging it as difficult and labeling it as sorrowful and there is a magnetic, energetic signature to those words. Sorrowful, sad, difficulties, they all have a vibrational signature. Every person that has ever spoken those words has given it more power and more energy. It creates an energetic river, so to speak, with a very strong magnetic pull. When you think of that word, difficulty, think of how many people have said that word "I'm having difficulties" or "it's difficult to do this" or "I can't do that because it's too difficult."

Every spoken word has power that does not disappear, energy does not disappear. Energy is forever, energy is eternal, so when you are in the midst of an experience let's say, and let's not give it the label, it's an experience, you look at what's happening around you there may be people crying, there may be a loved one that has passed and their body may be laying in state at the front of the room. You look around at the circumstances and you have a human feeling in your heart of how greatly you're going to miss that person. That is true, you will not be seeing that person, you will not be experiencing their company on this earthly plane any longer. However, there is a misconception that humans buy into that says, if I loved someone, I must pay the price with inconsolable grief. That is all a judgment. It is simply not true.

Let's think of another situation that might be happening. You sit with the bills in front of you and your checkbook to the right and the balance in your checkbook is far less than the amount that the bills add up to. You are hit with the overwhelming feeling of not enough. You judge yourself for creating this situation and you judge yourself for not creating enough abundance. There is lack in the checkbook and there are difficulties and stresses in the envelopes full of bills. The truth of the matter is, that the beating of yourself in that moment, the rendering of clothing and the gnashing of your teeth, because of the situation before you, changes the situation not at all. You can be in the moment observing what is and having all of the human feelings that are so magnetic and so common, because there have been so many, in that same kind of moment in time, creating the river that is named lack and too many bills and not enough. That river is flowing, that energetic river of thoughts and words is flowing and you either dive into that river and let it carry you to despair, or you stand on the edge of the river that is full of all of those bills and all of the bottom line of your checkbook and you observe it without judgment. You make whatever strides that you can make, perhaps dividing what is in the checkbook between the different bills. You observe the situation and you might introduce the thought of well shoot, this is what it is.

You might think to yourself, well I've been here before and I made it through and no one can take away my birthday! I'm standing here alive, breathing in and breathing out, my heart is beating, I have all of that going for me! You do the best that you can. If you are able to look and find the energy of opportunity, or find the energy of expectation, that tomorrow is another day, that you have the ability to make another paycheck you are on the right track. The human wants to sit in that *moment and come up with a plan or solution. What we are suggesting to you, through this one, is that you do not have the ability to come up with the solution. You cannot see the path to making it past all of those bills, you have not got imagination that is great enough to figure out a path that you are able to entertain that it's even possible, that could change your vibrational output, but what you do have potentially, is the knowing that the universe can do anything. That all wonderful things are out there and you are as deserving of those wonderful things as anyone! You can have the knowing that your vibrational output is either going to create more <u>lack</u> or it's going to draw <u>abundance</u> towards you.*

If you can just take away the labels of the situation, of the not enough and the lack, do what you can do, in the moment, and then sit in the knowing, sit in the power of the imagination thinking, "I wonder what wonderful solution is going to come to me around this, what will the universe think up that will dig me out of this hole. The universe can drop miracles into your lap dear ones, but the energy of lack and the energy of trying to figure out what can I do, how can I do it different, that energy pushes the universe away. Sitting in the knowing that it is possible for miraculous things to happen, <u>that</u> is the definition of faith. And when you get yourself into the vibrational vicinity of hope, of expectation, of wonder and awe for the next wonderful thing that is coming down the road, then the next wonderful thing can come. That is how you create your own reality, we know it is not easy dear ones, we know that it is elusive even, but this is the way that it is done.

Try to monitor the words that you say, try to release from your vocabulary the limiting words that you say repeatedly. Look at the vibrational signature of the words that come out of your mouth. Use the words that come out to create what you want, not to describe what you have, not to judge what you have as reality. This is real, you are saying, this is my reality. Yes, if you want more of it, keep talking about it, keep thinking about it, keep looking at it, but if you want something different, if you want to enjoy the magnificence that this life has for you, settle into the present moment and do what you can do. We are not saying that action is not appropriate, if you are at your job, do your job with your whole heart, with as much joy and gratitude as you can muster. If you are just sitting in your home, appreciate and look around to find things to appreciate, appreciate the breath coming in and out of your body, appreciate that every breath comes with it potential, potential and possibility. This is the path for creation and we understand that we have not said anything new, we understand that humans are tipping their toes into this world of self-creation and manifestation. But you're not getting it right dear ones, so we say it yet again and we will continue to say it as long as you continue to ask the question of how do we be joyful...

Chapter Sixteen

Why Bad Things Happen

I am vigilant about what I give my attention to. I avoid watching the news and wander away from conversations about political issues or the most recent tragic event that has happened in our world. But occasionally I falter, I was recently drawn to a four part documentary that was incredibly upsetting. I do not know why I did not turn it off, for some reason I needed to know how it ended. The ending was terrible! Suffice it to say that it depicted some of the darkest aspects of humanity.

It ended just as it was time to go to bed. My husband and I always go to bed at the same time but on this night, I told him I needed some time before I went to sleep. So, he went in and went to bed, and I stayed out in the living room trying to release the negative, horrific onslaught that I had just experienced. I prayed and brought through light language to help me release what I needed to release. Enough so I could go to bed, I did not sleep well but I got through the night. When I got up in the morning, I sat down at my computer thinking that I would be speaking to the next angel in the second half of this book. But when I sat down, they very clearly said to me I needed to go into meditation and let them talk to me about the things that were in that show.

This is a difficult subject; I'm going to be honest and tell you that I did not like their explanation. But it is the truth. Understanding the reality of our world is not always easy. This is what they had to say.

The show that you watched last night was so upsetting to you. It makes your gentle, sensitive heart call out to the universe, "how can these atrocities happen to sweet, innocent, little ones?" We know that these kinds of things are happening every day, all around the world. Things that for you, seem unspeakable. When we came forward to the earth and life began, there were certain rules and circumstances that were decided upon to be part of the earthly experience. Linear time, duality, free will, these are some of the big components of the earthly experience. It was not known, at that time, the degree that humans would be able to take their ability to choose. It seems that there is no limit to the degree that some individuals can go, in the domination and wielding of power, in the yearning and attempt to make themselves feel better. We know how upsetting it was for you to watch that show Kelly. You avoid the news and conversations that have any kind of negative thread, you always have since you were a little girl. Protecting yourself from as much of the negativity in the world as you could, because it felt so very, very wrong and terrible to you. It was very painful and caused you distress.

It is a very difficult thing for you to understand Kelly. (It just doesn't make sense to me) *we know it doesn't dear one, but nonetheless the souls that came forth have had lots of choices in their coming forward. You've already known and established, that you had picked your parents, so when the little soul decided to come forward and be a girl, born into that cult, there was a knowing that the path would be difficult. There was free will within her, some chose submission and others chose rebellion. We know you are not liking this Kelly; we know that it is difficult for you and your human, sensitive, heart to understand.*

We have previously spoken to you using the word atrocities, and you were able to accept the download around that. But with such vivid pictures in your mind from the show, it is much more difficult. We know it is not what you want to hear dear one, but we really must explain again that it does not impact us on this side, it does impact the evolution of the individual soul. As you spoke yesterday to Debbie, you cannot know light without dark. When you really pull back, there are many stories that help humans to understand the circumstances on the earth. It is when you get so specific in your mind, that you begin to flounder. Accept the knowing that we give you and know that love would never hurt, love would never do the atrocities. But love would incarnate into those situations as both perpetrator and victim. There are no victims in this world, though we know that it is a very difficult thing for you to understand. It is acting out a play for the lessons and the learnings to take place, for the strength to be gathered, for the resolve to be established. It is a loving act to come forward as a perpetrator for the evolution of the other. This is a very deep conversation Kelly, very difficult for the human to understand.

Narration-difficult to say the least! They have been working to help me understand this concept almost since the beginning of my ability to channel. It is very difficult, I have never experienced anything that would be considered an atrocity. I know that their intention behind this is for us to be able to understand… years ago, as a Christian woman defending her faith, I would often be asked,"why does God let bad things happen?" I was never able to answer that question. As painful as it is to understand, and wrap my mind around, this explanation does make sense. My prayer is that it will be a blessing to those who read it.

You are asking some very basic questions; you ask if you are part of a bigger soul. It is so difficult to explain because we are all energy, we are all One. Yes, there is a wave or a delineation of the whole, that you could consider that Kelly, came from. Each incarnation that you come forth with, evolves the soul with learnings, to come to that point of all knowing, then choose what you will do at that time. It is all true Kelly, all the things are true, the different stories that have been told to humans, to help them understand their existence, it all has some truth in it, it's all truth.

It is very difficult for you Kelly, step as far out as you can and let your voice go. It is important for you to learn to distinguish between the various ones that come through, because we do have access to different information. Let us speak, your mind is going quickly this morning. Let us speak of the sorrow that you felt in your heart as you thought of the situation with that clan in Utah and Texas. It is not that we condone the behaviors, that with your duality and your emotions, you have deemed unfit and horrific. We do not condemn it either. It is more of a knowing that the ultimate outcome is going to be for the greater good. The soul within the little girls, that you feel such pain around, was not hurt Kelly. It was only this incarnation, and you, with your linear understanding of time, think that they suffered so long from the abuse that you see. Remember dear one, that it is all happening now. The perspective of your soul looking down so to speak, being aware of the infinite number of incarnations, across all timelines and dimensions, that are happening in this one moment. You begin to get a perspective. They are unlimited, infinite, all happening at once, that is the perspective of the oversoul. That is our perspective.

The process that we have been helping you with, along with your team of angels and guides, can have a rippling effect across time and dimensions. There is great power in the present moment, for if there was a part of your oversoul let's say, it is a term that helps you to understand, if there is a part that is you, and frankly there is, being the perpetrator __and__ being the victim, and being all the roles, at all times, you can get a sense of the fact that you are all one. Yes, indeed it is mind blowing. But you, in this moment, with your deliberate intent, can affect it all. It is like cells in an organism, if the cells are all working together, as many as can for the common good, the entire organism will be affected. The goal of the universe, the goal of creation is love Kelly. You can know 100%, of the time these experiences create opportunities for humans to find their way back to love. If it does not in __this__ incarnation, know that there are infinite numbers of other incarnations to come into. The vibration of distress is far removed from the vibration of love. When you looked at the situation and felt such horror and distress, you had no love in your heart for the situation, you struggled to let us even say the word perpetrator, but that is the journey Kelly. Find love in your heart, as Jesus said on the cross, "forgive them, they know not what they do." It is a very complex situation for you to understand.

You are asking why we would have you understand it. The more of you who can find your way to neutrality, to non-judgment of any situation, no matter how atrocious it seems to you at the time, the greater the effect on the vibrational signature of humanity. Lower the veil of knowing over the situation, those situations tend to garner strong negative emotion from the human. The more of you who learn to control your emotional output, the more that will be intentionally added to the overall vibrational output of the planet, which is the purpose. We do not say it will be easy Kelly, it will be difficult, try to find some way to see the situations through the eyes of knowing.

You are asking us for a process to switch your mind, when you feel the judgments and the negative emotions begin to rise. You can state to yourself, "I can see this situation through the eyes of Source, and I can trust Source to work it out to its highest good". Because that is exactly what is happening in that moment. Then when you add to the power of the statement with "all souls in this moment, across all timelines and all dimensions, in all realms," it creates a powerful stance that will indeed have a rippling effect, that will potentially calm the waters of the situation at hand and beyond. It is the negative energetic blast that carries and expands the energetic signature of the situation. For you to be able to see the specifics and be able to turn it over to Source. You do not need to think about it in your human form, you do not need to take the energy of it in, you can be the bridge who immediately hands the situation over to the higher beings that are at play in the situation, Source Energy, God, angels, guides, however you would like to speak of it.

For example, if we take a bad situation and put it on a desert island. Pretend there's 1000 people experiencing the atrocity. But there is no outside observation. There is no righteous outcry of horror as the situation is observed. The situation is much smaller and has a much smaller energetic print in the cosmos, and in the beingness that is Mother Earth and all her children. There is a much smaller vibrational ripple shall we say. When you shine the light of media and the internet and spoken word over and over through generations and generations, we will use the example of the Holocaust, the ripple is so much farther reaching. You are asking if some good came from learning about the Holocaust, we would say to you that yes, there are those who, in their knowing found their way to love and compassion. We say to you dear one, that any eyes that are shined upon anything with knowing, observing and then the strong emotional response, it makes the energetic mud puddle of that issue bigger, in the energetic field of the human race. That is difficult for you, because humans have wanted to tell the story of the Holocaust with their passion and their grief, and their judgment and they have wanted to stand on the pulpit of learning and moving forward doing something different. That is not how it works.

We do celebrate you turning your face away from the atrocities; it is not necessarily the goal to stand with one's hands on one's hips staring into the face of the atrocities and not being moved. That is not the human condition. Avoid them as you will, but when one is presented to you Kelly, or to any of the people who may read these words, trust it in the universe's hands. Know that there are beings, angels, guides, non-physical helpers who are very active in supporting all in the situation. The human does not need to understand the far-reaching implications and the less attention that you give it and the less emotion that you give it, other than compassion and love, not pity, the better. Compassion and love for all involved, that will create less of an imprint on the energetic field.

Draw your own energy in Kelly, when there is the opportunity to judge, so that you do not leave your energy in a situation. You do not want to share your energetic field with these situations that we are talking about. Call your energy back daily. Because humans do lose parts of their energetic field when they have an emotional response to a situation. That is how the handprints get on your energetic field, because humans do strew their energy about. That is as good a way to explain it as any. So consciously ask Mothers Earth's help with this and the help of all your guides and teachers and all the universes. Ask Father, Mother, God, to help you call back to yourself all the energy that belongs with you in this moment, across all moments, across all dimensions, across all timelines, in all realms.

Chapter Seventeen

Vibrational Housework

It is very human to have a bad day. Often, we have no idea why we are feeling off or out of balance. But we are, we may be feeling grumpy, we may be feeling a little depressed and we can't put our finger on why. Oftentimes it is just a matter of going to bed at night, getting a good night's sleep and starting again tomorrow and we feel better. It's a new day, a new start and we're feeling more like ourselves. This is exactly how I have lived my life. Until my guides explained to me how important it is to keep our energy bodies clean.

Let's do this housekeeping before we begin our day, let's settle into ourselves and ask our angel team, ask our higher self, to come within us and take everything away that is not serving our highest good. You don't need to be specific; you don't need to know what is hanging around in your energy field making you not feel good. It can just be your daily practice of cleaning your energy field out. For example, today you may pick up a small piece of energy that is clinging to you. It might be called self-worth or self-image or any of the things that humans get tied up with, when you walk into a room, or you walk through a store, know that it's magnetized. If you walk by someone who has that same issue, by the magnetic force, it will be drawn to you and will create more and more of the negative energy that is clinging to you. Then that negative energy will activate a human emotion and you're going to start feeling off or you're going to feel depressed or you're going to feel blue, and you don't even really know why. It is that energetic baggage that you are picking up along your path, you very easily can take care of that. Humans just don't know that they need to. You need to do it every day, like brushing your teeth.

Let's use the example of being in a crowd, perhaps at a party. If you have been invited to this party you must know people there, some are friends, some people you don't know at all. Most people have a certain level of nervousness going into any of these kinds of situations. Remember that any thought, word, or emotion is energy. Energy, once it's created, never goes away. As a person is a bit nervous getting ready for the party, these little snags of negative energy are clinging to and hanging around their energy field. Such as, "I look fat in this dress" or "I hope Sally is not there, I know she does not like me" Most people at that party will have those similar snags. Remember it's not the words, it is the energetic signature of the words. Self-worth, feelings of inadequacy...I'm seeing them in my mind's eye like a little dark spot on the outside of our energy bubble. As we walk by someone who has the same kind of dark spot on the outside of their energy bubble there is an exchange of energy. The spot on my bubble got bigger and the spot on that person's bubble got bigger.

Remembering the law of attraction, we know that like attracts like. These little mud puddles of negative energy cling to us as we move through the crowd. If you are an empath, you may even be aware as you walk by someone that they have a "negative vibe". But not all people are empaths. That does not mean that they do not experience energy, it just means they are not as aware of it. This exchange of energy is common to all humans. Once you understand this, it is very easy to take care of it. Before I describe the different methods I have been given to do that, I want to speak about humans and their moods. It is so common for humans to experience emotions without having any idea why they are feeling the way they are feeling. What I have been discussing is true for people who are on their spiritual awakening path or for people who are living completely in their human condition and have no idea about energy, it affects everyone. The negative thought that runs through our head, the show we watch on TV that resonates with us on an emotional level, so many things create energy, and the negative energy needs to be dealt with.

What my guides have explained to me, is that we don't need to get to the point of the bad mood. If we get in the habit of routinely cleaning our energy fields, we are going to see a remarkable difference in how we feel overall. Sometimes we know why we're mad, someone did something that pissed us off. But why are we angry? Why does anyone have the power to make us angry? The short answer is, they don't. When any emotion has been triggered in a human, it is because of the energetic signature of what is going on. If you look at the situation that made you angry and you do a bit of excavation, it rarely is what is happening on the surface.

Let's create an example, let's pretend that today you washed the kitchen floor. You shined it all up pretty and you feel good about your efforts. Then someone comes home, a partner or a child perhaps, and they walk with their muddy shoes across your floor. You become angry, you're angry because they tracked up your clean floor! But the truth of the matter is, that is not what you're angry about. Let's do some of the excavation, there is that inner self that is saying, "If they valued me at all they would never have done that!" "If they had any respect for me they would not have done that." So that must mean you do not deserve respect, you are not valuable... you are not worthy. All of that is energy. All that hangs in your energetic field until it is taken care of. It is why some people feel that they are always being dumped on, or people are always disrespecting them, and the list could go on and on. It is because they are carrying the energetic signature of all those emotions and beliefs. It draws more of the same by its magnetic force to you. The following is my guides' explaining these principles to me and giving me some concrete strategies to use to clean up energy.

To be able to be in a space of self-love and self-care, what an interesting concept to think of after an interaction, after a gathering, after an event. Before much time has passed, to sit oneself down and say, "Let's look within and see if there is anything that we need to take care of? Is there anything that needs to be processed and released?" Because if it's in your energetic psyche, it's connecting to your emotions and giving you those off feelings, those unbalanced feelings. That is what gets your attention, your feelings. Wouldn't it be interesting if you could step over that hurdle and have these processes that you know and use out of self-care and self-love? Make it a part of your day, to just sit with oneself and ask, "Have you picked up any energies along your path that we need to take care of?" Then trust that we will bring those things to the surface. Reach to your higher self and look at what you are holding and let us do that internal housekeeping before it has time to give you the bad day or makes you snap and growl at someone, or develop the physical manifestation of the headache or the stomachache or the pain. People have no idea that they need to recover from certain things. There needs to be a recovery method that people practice routinely when they have been in contact with many people or certain situations...

You may have globs of mud on the outside of your energy. It might not be very big, and it might not be very problematic but when you get into a crowd of people or when a circumstance comes to you problems may develop. Every circumstance is made up of threads of energy, different colors, different vibrational threads of energy. Every experience is made-up of all these different threads of energy and there might be only one small thread that matches that muddy print that's on the side of your energy field but it's going to magnetize itself together and it's going to make that dark print a little bigger, a little darker, until finally that energy mud puddle on the side of your energy field is big enough to cause the bad day or the grumpy feeling with your loved one or the blues or whatever. It will rear its head because we are beings of light, and our natural state is pure positive energy. When we have those handprints in our energy field, we need them to be gone because we are meant to be pure positive energy. But we are not reaching in and doing the housekeeping that needs to be done. It needs to be done daily. Or maybe frequently, don't get carried away with the shoulds, but it does need to be done often. So, sit down after a particular time when you know that a circumstance might be difficult, for instance a family gathering or a meeting with someone. We can look at situations and know they have familiar vibrational threads embedded within them. Take a minute when you come out of that meeting or gathering and sit with it and ask yourself, "is there anything I need to clean up? Is there anything I need to let go of? I want to connect to the love of the universe and run that love through my energy field." Just to consciously run the energy of universal love through your energy field with the intention of taking anything that doesn't serve you down to Mother Earth, clear that right out and take it down to Mother Earth and she is opening her arms and it's going to make the trees grow and the sunshine and it's all positive for her but it doesn't serve us in our energy field.

In the same way that you need to tend to your physical body daily with drinks of water and food, you need to tend to your energetic body with love and care. It is so simple, you can do it with a breath. Breathe in that universal love let it just bathe over you just because you can, because you need it in the same way that you need a drink of water. You need that beautiful flow of energetic love to go through your energy field and then it's not going to feel so crappy to walk through a store or to go to a meeting. It won't have so much of an effect on you because your energy is clean and not drawing other energies in.

Section Two,

The Angels

I have always believed in and trusted angels! I have called on them for love and support and safety since I was a small girl. Years ago, I participated in a class about angels. I remember it being lovely, and that the lady holding the class had wonderful energy. But I was still in the grips of my religious dogma and any conscious connection across the veil was frowned upon. We were allowed to pray of course, but to be empowered to have a personal relationship with a specific angel, knowing that you could call on that angel at any time and they would be with you, that was taboo. After that class I bought a book that the teacher recommended. I've never read the book. But I have held on to it. In my meditation this morning my guides reminded me of that book. They asked me to get the book and write the names of the different angels into this document that I am working on. They said just by writing their names into this book I would begin the creative process of inviting each one of them in to help me.

I have never spent any amount of time learning about specific angels. Of course, I have heard about them, I've seen references to Archangel Michael, or Archangel Raphael. But I have never developed a personal relationship with the specifics of the different angels. My guides knew that I did not have a personal relationship with the individual angels. I think up to this point I found it confusing. I would wonder how anyone could know the specifics! I guess now I understand how that can happen lol!

I asked my guides what the benefit of knowing these specific things about the angels would be. They explained that there is great power in having a specific situation that is going on and knowing the angel who specializes in that kind of situation to call on. They told me that when I called out for angelic support in general, I absolutely was supported. I knew that I had felt the love and presence of my angels all my life. But my guides explained that each angel is a collective of energy. We can have a personal relationship with each of those collectives. I have always known that to have angelic help you needed to ask. I understand now that when you ask with a specific intention, knowing the name to invoke, it creates a greater connection. It facilitates the interaction between the angel and the human.

This is new for me, I'm very comfortable now talking with my guides and bringing them through and transcribing their information. But the idea of specifically reaching out to an entity, an angel no less, and inviting them in for a conversation is new. However, I trust my guides, I know they do not introduce me to concepts that I'm not ready for. So, my friends, we will be meeting the angels together. I am excited at the thought!

I set down one morning with the intention of inviting in Angel Ariel. She is the first angel in the list.I was struggling with the idea of being able to channel different entities consciously, that demon named self-worth or worthiness reared its ugly head and I was struggling. I had what I would call a full on spiritual anxiety attack! The following is the process they took me through, it was beautiful!

You are struggling with the idea of being able to shift easily between different entities, different collectives. To be able to take one of the names of the angels and just key into that angel and get actual information. (I know it boils down to worthiness, I just don't feel worthy, why should **I** be able to do that!?)

Humans experience these challenges of self often. You might hit that kind of moment that is holding you back and ask yourself what is this really? When you sat with us this morning and you heard the YouTube video say that you all have these abilities, this is something you're aware of Kelly. We have been bringing through this concept to you, though it is not landing fully in your knowing, it is out on the periphery. It's an idea that your mind is trying to wrap around. You got to the point of being able to acknowledge that you are holding that knowing away. You're familiar with us and our processes, and our bringing you forward and helping you to develop. You're familiar enough with that to know there is something holding you back. We are coaxing you ahead, but you have something that is stuck. This is a beautiful opportunity for us to work with you and yes even give you a process for your book!

It is overwhelming to you, as you listen to the words that we are saying you are thinking,"I don't have any idea what they're going to say" and that's right you don't. That is part of the hurdle Kelly. You get stuck when you think that we are going to truly bring through things that you absolutely don't know. We have been able to do that many, many times. Bringing through the Mother Earth transmission, bringing through so many transmissions that we brought to you and you were able to receive.

But we almost must sneak them in through the side when you land in your human mind.

You say for instance you want information; you want to connect with a specific angelic collective and you have no idea what Angel Ariel is all about. You have no frame of reference for that at all, so you get scared, and you get overwhelmed, because with all our experiences together it is not us you do not trust, it is yourself. Let us ask ourselves together, let us work through this with you. What is it <u>really</u>? What is it <u>really,</u> that is making it so difficult to think that with all that you know, with all that you've experienced, you do not think you can just drop into your heart, open your mind, and allow Angel Ariel to come through you. Even as you speak those words it feels uncomfortable to you, let us ask again, why? Breathe into your heart and ask why. Why do you think it's not possible for you?

"It goes to worthiness; why am I worthy to be able to do these things, why am I having all of these awesome experiences and other people aren't?"

You are seeing yourself through the lens of humanness Kelly. Remember that all time is now. This present moment is aligned with <u>all</u> present moments, in <u>all</u> dimensions, in <u>all</u> timelines. The conscious, deliberate work that you do in this moment will have a rippling effect on all the moments. That just seems so fantastic to you that you're struggling with it. Let's say it again, your mind is going to what ifs, how is that possible? It's a big concept Kelly, it's a big concept. Let's just go with it right now and we will continue on. Your human mind needs a cookie in the corner! (My mind was running in circles!) *Let us just speak to you dear one, you are so afraid of making a mistake. Every mistake you ever have made and every mistake you're ever going to make, the energy of that is in <u>this</u> moment. Let's look at what it means to make a mistake.*

Go to your inner child, the thought of being wrong, having your words not listened to, having really good ideas and being discounted by people, that landed in your little heart Kelly. It landed in your little heart and put an energetic imprint that is still there. There are many layers to this process Kelly. The process we want for you right now is the one that will be easy to share with your readers. It will also have the greatest impact on you. You know that <u>is</u> how it works. Let us go back to the beginning. You are struggling to think that you can reach out to Angel Ariel and ask questions and get true answers because you do not feel worthy. It is another layer of that worthiness that is deep inside of you.

Drop deep into your heart, breathe into your heart the knowing of the concept of worthiness. Breathe into your mind and into your headspace, the concept of worthiness. When you breathe in, you would bring in an explosive power into any memory, breathe in the power of the universe to fragment and dislodge and loosen in all areas, in all dimensions. (They are guiding me to take big loud breaths in) *You breathe into your psyche, you breathe into all dimensions, you breathe into all paths on this earth, you breathe into past, present and future. You shake loose all the bits of unworthiness, all the memories, all the deep seated feelings that landed on hearts that were delicate and gentle and were hurt. You loosen all of that up that you can, with this beautiful, beautiful, explosive energy. You breathe in the strong, powerful, energy of your higher self, that can break this up, to bring this energy in and break this up! Swirl it outside of yourself in your energy body. Swirl that energy in that energy body and we will break up every memory, we break up the knowing, we break it up! We break it up! We break it up! We find it, we seek it out for you, you do not have to acknowledge the memories. Some memories you will ignore, but others you cannot. You can trust your higher self to go into your energy body, to go into your physical body, to go into your cellular structures. You invite the energy in, and you ask it to pull out by the roots, to explode and fragment all these memories of unworthiness. Memories of you not being enough, you break that up and you swirl that energy until you feel, you feel the swirling energy within yourself.*

Narration-the energy was building within me at this point, I could feel the energy swirling. I was feeling overtaken by the energy but I trusted…

Then you bring in that cosmic energy of light down through top of your head, you open your mind, open your heart, open your chakras, you open. Open with your intention and you ask for the color. What color will come in for you? (They are saying that you ask the light what color are you? I believe it may be different each time) *right now the red and the pink energy is swirling like a vortex, like a tornado coming into your energy field as your hand goes with the energy.* (They cued me to use my hands to swirl the energy) *swirling, swirling the energy and it is picking up, it is picking up and drawing to that beautiful pink and red energy as it comes through your energy body, as it comes through your physical body, your cellular body, on all dimensions, on all timelines, in this moment we proclaim that we are releasing. Releasing these fragments of unworthiness, we release the fragments of unworthiness, the belief in* unworthiness, we release the belief that we are unworthy. We release in all dimensions and across all timelines, in all cellular bodies, and all physical bodies, in all esoteric bodies, all energetic bodies. We release that belief, we release any beliefs that do not support our highest good, for where we are in this moment in time, we release it.

The human would just sit and roll that energy, roll that energy, letting the time flow, letting their mind wander to any point in time, any memory that might contain any of this energy and they throw it into this swirling vortex of energy. You throw it out, you clean the trash, you press delete, you press clear the trash with your intention and it will swirl until you feel like it has collected all that it can collect. All that it can, in all dimensions, and all timelines, in all cellular structures, in all memories, in all physical structures, energetic structures, you swirl it until you feel like it has collected all that it possibly can. Then you state to the cosmos, "I Kelly Coleen Bowker, state to the universe, that I release feelings of unworthiness. I step into the glory that is me, I step into my connection with all non-physical beings with my intention, my strength, my resolve, and my sovereignty, in this moment. I step into the knowing that I am worthy, and I am thankful for that beautiful vortex of energy that has collected all the remnants of anything that does not serve me. Anything that's not for my highest good, in all the timelines and dimensions and with my sovereignty, I send it down to Mother Earth to be alchemized."

With gratitude to Mother Earth, thank you for the support, thank you that I know you are nothing but blessed by this offering that I send to you. Knowing you support me in my journey Mother Earth, that you walk hand in hand with me, connected through the love bond that is between me and you, as I am one of your children, I am part of you, to release once and for all, to release to the degree that this moment is able to release for my highest good at this time.

You will not go backwards dear one, but there is never ever an end to the amount of your worth. So, as your worthiness in this moment is established, in the next moment it is greater, it is more. In any moment in time, if you have picked up along your energetic path energies that grab onto you, that play in your mind and make you feel less than or bring up that feeling of unworthiness again, you will do this process again, that is right. This is part of your earthly journey Kelly, coming into your worthiness, coming into your sovereignty.

The only time that you will struggle to align with your worthiness is when you step out of the present moment. That is when *humans think of this distant thing they want to accomplish, then doubts and questions about their worthiness to accomplish such a thing will come into their minds.*

 This was incredibly powerful! I felt the energy move through my body and out again. And when it was done, I felt humble and worthy. So blessed to be doing this work with them. Knowing that when it was time to connect with the angels, I would be able to. Notwithstanding the fact that the concept blew my mind!

Angel Ariel

Let Angel Ariel speak. We have been with you always Kelly, we have been with you always. We are the angels of the chakras, we are a team, and we work with the energy system that the humans have. There is wonderful power and knowledge in this. This is why I came through first, to bring the frequency of knowing to you, so I Ariel am the Angel of knowing, the Angel of Oneness, the Angel of worthiness, because knowing is all-encompassing, when you know you're one with all that there is, there is nothing that you do not possess, there is nothing that you do not have the ability to access. The ability to know, Angel Ariel, Angel Ariel, when you speak our name, it will bring reminders.

When you sit in the beautiful energy that is us, that is Angel Ariel, yes Kelly, you are here with us. When you connect with Angel Ariel, you are connecting to the <u>knowing</u> of your worthiness, the <u>knowing</u> of your sovereignty. Allow us in, call our name for the reminder, Angel Ariel, and we will bathe you in the knowingness that you are divine, that you are one with all that is, that you hold within the very DNA of your body, the ability to be one with all that is. Within the oneness, that is also part of us, part of our teaching, part of our frequency, within that is the knowingness that you are One with everything. To be able to bring Angel Ariel into the moment, as you look at your beautiful world and have us sprinkle our beautiful energy into that moment. Bonding the energy that is you, in your human form, with the energy of what you are looking at. Yes, we are Angel Ariel, you feel our energy, you feel the difference. Sit with the energy, feel it in your body, feel it in your hands and your face and your upper torso. We are the energy of the highest chakra the chakra of knowing we do align with the eighth chakra. Do not get into your mind Kelly, let us give you what we would have you know. What has gone before is it's own frequency. To touch those that it's meant to touch and even as you say that you acknowledge that you never did read that book, but the book gave you the names to begin with. There are many more of us than there are in that book, dear one.

Begin dear one, in the same way that you do when you bring through Lacroose. We are but another frequency that will come through you. Pull yourself out of your thinking mind my dear and allow us to come through in our way. The angelic realm is all around you, we always are. We are helpers in this dimension. We connect to humans through their chakra system. There is great facilitation that can happen with the utilization of the human's chakra system. It is a tool or a mechanism that

96

was gifted to humans. It is a mind-boggling experience for you humans when we come through with the clarity and the deliberateness that this kind of personal relationship can bring through. It is our greatest joy, our heart's greatest... We are not quite in sync yet my dear, for you to understand the words I am trying to express, but that will come in time.

You ask if it is important for you to be specific about your requests to the different angels that you are going to be meeting. We work together certainly, there is a collaboration of energy. But there is an advantage to knowing the specific frequency and personality...it is a close word but not quite what we're wanting to say, the specific nuances, these specific gifts and skills and areas of expertise that is it exactly! Each collective angel has an area of expertise. Mine as Angel Ariel is the area of knowing. You have been quite receptive to my whisperings as you have opened, I have been able to give you many various knowings that have facilitated your path with your guides and the various entities that are working with you, to facilitate you. Your mind fills with questions as we say those words. Dear one step back, you need to simply feel us. Feel us moving on your body. Feel us on the surface of your skin, on the surface of your face, around your head. We facilitate the connection, we facilitate your ability to shift your energy into that oneness that is so advantageous for you.

Your guides and team, which your angels are a part of, have been working with you Kelly, and you're getting more deliberate in your connection with us. Do not for an instant think that we have not always been with you. You're asking if any of us are your guardian angel. The angelic realm is vast. It is all one as well, the energy of all, it doesn't matter the timeline or dimension, that energy is still all one. But is there a frequency that is different than the angel, that is the frequency of your chakras, that has been assigned to you from birth? The answer is yes indeed there is. You are correct when you feel that it is a more masculine energy because a great deal of the work of the guardian angel is safety. Angel Michael works collaboratively with the guardians to facilitate them. You ask if there is a hierarchy in the angelic realm at this time, we feel that that conversation can wait for a later time dear one. That's it sweetie, that is the question to ask, what is the question that I should ask Angel Ariel today, what does Angel Ariel have for me today.

Open your mind Kelly, say yes to the knowing that I will bring into your mind. The confidence as you move forward connecting to your various angels. Yesterday we worked on your releasing that thought that you are not worthy of this. Every human is worthy Kelly every human just does not find themselves in the vibrational vicinity to be able to allow it. There is no better than, there is no hierarchy in the humans either as you already know.

Yes, dear one, we did send you some of the light language. The light language or the language of light is exactly what it says, it is a tool for us in the other dimensions and in the other frequencies and realms, it is a vibration to bring in with it knowings and messages and enlightenments. It does indeed go into the human and unlock at the deepest level, which humans have referred to as the DNA level there is an aspect of that dear ones but we are facilitating that crystalline grid visual that we helped facilitate into your mind. The energy of the crystalline grid goes at such a deep and fine and high level within your physical makeup it is not a place, it is a frequency. And that the light language can open it, is as good of an understanding as any right now. It opens that ability to receive.

You want to be deliberate; you want to follow the rules that you believe that we are setting forth. When these messages come through Kelly, they are a blending for whatever the highest good at the time is. The individuation of the angels is a facilitator. We would like to leave it at that for now. The knowing that we want to give you, is the confidence in your ability to connect. For you to simply open and allow the different frequencies to come in. There will be a potential change in your voice and your delivery. This is difficult for you to allow; we are giving you the knowledge that you just can go with it. Judge all in your heart dear one, does the energy of me flowing through you with this message feel anything other than a blessing? No, it does not, (I'm sorry I doubt, I'm sorry I doubt... *Sweet girl, we do not want you to feel sad or guilty, step back and realize how difficult and broad this is! Feel our love for you Kelly, it has been such a joy watching you unlock your abilities.*

Narration-that is where Angel Ariel stoped. I did indeed bring through all of the angels that I reached out to. The top half of the chakra angels came through to me without revealing their colors. I think this is because that is the part of the energy system that I'm the most connected with. I've always been very focused on spiritual development, but my connection to Mother Earth needed work. I did not need to utilize the frequencies of the colors to facilitate the angels to come through until Angel Cassiel, who is the angel of the third chakra instructed me to. When she came through, she explained the importance of the colors and

98

asked me to put the colors and the associated body parts into each section.

Angel Raphael

Do not get confused with the voice and the difference. There will likely come a time when we will come through sounding all very similar Kelly. It is not wrong for you to direct your attention to the chakra that you are imagining I am a part of. We are a frequency. We are Angel Raphael and yes you have met us before as you enjoyed the beautiful meditation with our dear friend who works with us solely. (There is a lady on YouTube who channels angel Raphael and has channeled him for the last 30 years. She is wonderful!)

The energy that is Raphael is vast, we are the crown chakra, we are the opening that comes, the ability for the opening. We bring to your mind the energy she so often is bringing through, feel the energy on your crown chakra, yes, we have opened it, do you feel it? Yes, indeed you do! We have now brought it in, and you feel the difference in energy do you not? We are the gatekeeper of the energy body of the human. We are the ones who help to regulate what comes in and unlocks. We have been busy with you, young lady, we have facilitated much of what has gone on. You always have been, by your very nature, quite open to the cosmos and the esoteric realm. You feel the energy of Angel Ariel hovering just above my energy and that is exactly right, but it is also a blending that is used often. I work with Angel Ariel to create the ideal circumstance, so to speak, in the opening of the individual, the softening of their resolve.

You were asking what to put in your book about Angel Raphael. When you are struggling as you have been Kelly. When you are struggling to allow the vastness of the energy to come in (God in heaven if it's vaster then I have already experienced I don't think I can take anymore!) *Yes, dear one, it is us that facilitates that. We are the gatekeeper that allows the energy to flow at the rate that is for the highest understanding. That is right dear one, we will ask to speak it will facilitate your understanding, just step back as far as you can to allow, say yes.*

In understanding the Angel Raphael, there is a need to understand the energy body. The energy body surrounds the individual. The word gatekeeper is an adequate description for the energy of Angel Raphael. We tend to the comings and goings. We vibrate closely with the individual stretching, opening, that connection to your higher self. We work closely with your team. You just thought about the mediumship readings, and you are right Kelly, it is a very small aspect of what we are talking about. Humans have the need for validation, to get access to their loved ones is a wonderful thing but in the scope of what you now have access to, it is a very small needle in a very large haystack. We do not value it less, it is a tool that helps to unlock the average human's ability to understand and yes that's where Angel Raphael comes in, it is through the crown chakra, the chakra that's at the top of your head. It is through that the knowings can come. Often it would be through something like a psychic experience or a mediumship experience that can validate and bring evidence to the average human. That is a part of what we do.

Narration-this makes so much sense! Because to blend with the energy of someone who has passed away you have to open, now I realize the opening is the crown chakra I never really put that together before. So, Angel Raphael facilitates the readings by assisting when we ask to open our chakra.

We have given you the picture of the key and the lock. That is a concept that we would have you bring to your readers. To call on Angel Raphael is to ask for angelic assistance in opening your mind, your psyche, your everything. To be the key that will open and allow the knowings and the information and relationships, there's such a vastness of this interactive relationship between the human and the other realms and dimensions. So yes, dear girl, we are saying we are the angel of the key to opening. We are the gatekeepers, and we are the key to the gate. We have the discernment to know what energies will be most effective for whatever the human is experiencing at any particular time. An antenna so to speak that the human utilizes to bring in what is needed at any given time. We also keep our finger on the pulse of how much is appropriate, how open the individual should be. You ask about the understanding that you have of the chakras becoming too open or too closed or blocked in some way. That is correct dear ones. The angels of the chakras can utilize the energy of the chakra to facilitate the life and development of the human that we are interacting with. However, there is the energetic work, that when the human becomes aware of and spends some conscious time as we discussed yesterday with you the cleaning of the energetic field and the deliberate balancing of the chakras creates a much more favorable environment for us to work in.

We would speak to you on balancing your chakras. Yesterday we spoke through Ariel. Remember we are all one, but we do have our areas of expertise so to speak, we are all present right now Kelly, even those you have yet to meet, who look forward to meeting you and speaking through you so let us speak.

Yesterday we talked at length and gave you processes to clean your energetic field which we might remind you that you have yet to do this morning. It does not take a great deal of time dear one it takes your intention. Humans want to make things so complex. But you are incredibly powerful beings, humans think that there needs to be great long meditations utilizing colors and frequencies and body systems and all the things that yes, are all valuable. We do not say that anything is better or worse, you have learned that, you know that very clearly now. What we do say is this, in the same way Kelly Coleen, that you can truly shift and speak to and through and with Angel Raphael, just as easy as shifting your mind and speaking my name, you can balance your chakras. Let us bring to your mind dear one, please step back out of the way, we have a method for you, we have a process for you to share.

It takes a working knowledge which you will have when you have completed this process with the angels. It takes a working knowledge to balance the chakras. You must have your feet on the ground figuratively, meaning start by connecting to Mother Earth. By sending Mother Earth love, sending it down into Mother Earth just with your intention, you send energy and love down to Mother Earth you connect. Then you send energy and love to the cosmos to All that there is. Then you ask your angels to balance and clear your chakras to bring them into perfect harmony, that is the best for what you need to accomplish today. You ask for your chakras to be balanced across all timelines, all dimensions across all realms and frequencies. You are learning to do the work in this present moment will affect all.

Narration-There are no words to explain what they are showing me, they are communicating with me more and more through telepathy, it is very difficult to explain. Basically, the work we do in the present moment can reach into the past and into the future. That's exactly what they're telling me! This telepathy thing is a pain in the ass!

We understand that dear one, however if you were just hearing words would you have a true understanding?

(No, I probably wouldn't. Can you recap for me?)

Yes, after you have cleared your energy with the process that we gave you yesterday of gathering any cling-ons, any energies in your field that are not serving you. Use that process to break them up, gather them up and send them down to Mother Earth. Then you send your love and your appreciation and your gratitude for your wonderful connection to

Mother Earth. Then you send your energy up to the cosmos with gratitude and love and the support that you are being given from all realms and dimensions which are contributing to your process and your evolution. Then you ask your angels to balance, to adjust, to bless and attune all your chakras to your highest good. Bringing them into the resonance that is for your highest good. Bringing them into the frequency that is for your highest good for all time, across all timelines and all frequency and all dimensions and all realms. Across all planes of existence, past, present and future, to the left and to the right, in all directions from this moment on, you ask that they balance for your highest good. You breathe that energy of balance knowing that your angels have done the work and you step forward into your day empowered, knowing that you are ready for the next level of knowing that you will have. It is like tilling the garden Kelly, this process is making you prepared and stable for life and for enlightenment and evolution. It also creates the ability for you to be able to resonate and shine the light of your love into the crystalline grid.

That is where Angel Raphael ended. This certainly is an incredible journey. I have no idea if each Angel will bring through its own process for us or not, but these first two certainly have been wonderful and enlightening and empowering! I'm really beginning to get a feel for how they want us to interact with them. They are helping us no matter what, but when we deliberately and consciously attuned to them we are creating a much more powerful connection.

Color-violet

Body parts-pituitary, cerebral cortex, central nervous system.

Angel Gabriel

Angel Gabriel, Angel Gabriel, I just read your name in this document, and I felt the energy. I am feeling it moving down my body. So, Angel Gabriel you are the Angel of the third eye.

Yes, by-gori, this is Angel Gabriel! I am the angel of the third eye, being able to see and receive and perceive in realms that are different then the realm you are used to, that is what the third eye is all about. I am part of this collective of angels, I work together with this team, supporting all humans as they strive to see what it is to have the second site so to speak, that people have spoken of many times. It is the gateway to your intuition. It is the most direct route to being able to receive minute by minute guidance throughout your day.

Remember our friend, that the chakra system, though it has been broken into individual parts, is one beautiful energetic body within and around the human. It is associated with body systems and there is value to that knowing. When Angel Rafael spoke of streamlining the balancing process, we in no way wanted to diminish the connection to color and to body systems and frequencies, all of that is very valuable. What we are bringing forward in these processes that we are giving to you at this time, is a more expedited or streamlined approach to things. We are working on the assumption that people will practice these things on a regular basis. There may come times when the situation warrants a more thorough or deeper dive, so to speak, into any of the processes that we are giving you. We want to speak at this time from that place of the intuitive knowing of what is needed. That is part of what the third eye chakra represents. It is that intuitive knowing of what resonates with you. What is right for you at this time? We are the energy that draws you into a particular YouTube video and gives you that feeling of knowing that this is right for you and your development currently. We also give you the discordant sensation that something is not right for you.

So let us speak to those who choose a path perhaps like the one that you travelled in your younger years, when you were a very devout Baptist Christian girl. Let us speak to that path. There is great appeal to some for the rules and the directions, the very specific rights and wrongs that are laid out by the one standing in the front of the church. They get great comfort in following the rules, for whatever has happened in their lifetime that has brought them to this place, this place of knowing. When the individual incarnated the circumstances of their life were such that it created within them a need to trust something outside of themselves.

They are given many opportunities along their path. All people who travel those paths have these opportunities, but it is what resonates with them. It is correct for them. It is difficult for you to understand this because you feel so free, having broken the chains that religious life had for you. But those chains create comfort for some Kelly, it resonates with them, and their love and devoutness are as much in alignment with their soul's development as your current path is for you. You ask how that can be true. There are concepts dear one, that are beyond your grasp in this moment. Suffice it to say that the knowing that you have, that we gave you previously, that everyone is on the correct path for them, is true and correct. When you think about it too deeply, you begin to get confused, but you resonate with the knowing that there is no <u>wrong</u> path. There is no right and wrong Kelly. There are limitless experiences and limitless amounts of journeys into this realm of experience. We Angel Gabriel through your third eye chakra, your sixth chakra, assist the human with discernment. The more personal the relationship between you and that which is us, the clearer the discernment will be.

Let us talk about what discernment means. Discernment is specific to the individual. You are not discerning what is right for all, you are discerning what is right for you, in this moment and it is true that what could be right for you and good for you in this moment, could be different in a future moment or might have been different in a past moment. You discern and have clarity of thinking through your third eye. You settle into it when a situation or circumstance presents itself; you ask us, Angel Gabriel, to give you guidance and we will facilitate it through the third eye energy. It is how you navigate life. We are showing you the interrelationship of the eighth, seventh and sixth chakras. The broad knowings that come through Angel Ariel, the adjustment of the crown by Angel Raphael, letting in the correct amount through the adjustments of the openness of the crown and then to the discernment that will come through the third eye, realizing that this is all instantaneous. Your entire chakra system works in unison. You can consciously utilize these tools.

A process for developing your ability for discernment, is to look at a situation and shift your perception from the seeing eyes up to the third eye. When you give your attention to that space on the front of your forehead, between your eyebrows, it activates the third eye's abilities. You will have an energetic knowing about the circumstances that you are viewing. It gives you that 5th dimension view of oneness with what you are looking at. It is not so connected to your thinking mind. It is not so full of labels and there are no judgments. It gives you the perspective of being the observer which is a wonderful perspective to learn to practice in your incarnation. As often as you can be reminded to shift into that third eye perception it will benefit you greatly. It reminds you of one of the very first chapters in this book and the tool that we gave around being reminded to connect and take that breath, these are all wonderful processes.

The third eye process is also a wonderful process. You see as you look out the window, what the human mind would call the birch tree. When you are shifted into that third eye perspective you see it without the label, and you feel the oneness, the calling, the connection, it is a wonderful perspective. But now let us take it a step further. When you are out in the world and there are those coming in and out of your experience, there are energetic offerings coming to you and around you, it is the discernment of the third eye, if you can remind yourself to just have that perception for a moment, that will give you that wonderful sense of peace and knowing. It will lead you to or away from any given circumstance. You will feel an energetic resonance or pull in a certain direction, and you will learn to feel that energetic repellent feeling away from or pull toward any individual or circumstance or choice. Friends, utilize the third eye to navigate your life and know that you are loved, and we are with you.

Color-indigo/purple

Body parts-eyes, pineal gland, and face

Angel Celestina

Let us speak through you dear one. In the writing of the names into your document you began the process of drawing us through and as our dear brethren and sister have spoken, we are a team we work as one. Though you feel us separately with the specificity of each of our gifts and helping ability, we are all here Kelly. When you think about yourself and what a path you have been on, searching and studying spirituality and things of this nature for years and years and yet the power of the chakra system has never resonated with you. It is an important tool that humans have access to. It can be wielded in a much more deliberate way.

I am Angel Celestina. I am the angel of the throat chakra, which means I am the angel of the spoken word. I am the angel of the written word and the thought words, I am the angel of words. As you can imagine the connection with me is a challenging one for humans. Though I am here to facilitate you with all the love of the universe at my disposal radiating out, it is difficult for humans to hear my whisperings. Because the spoken word, the expression of oneself, is what I am the angel of. You struggle dear one because it is so easy to confuse the ego mind with the whispering of the angels or your higher self. This is certainly a challenge. There is great power, as you know, in the spoken word. You did a lovely job the other day explaining the power and energy component of words and how they are made up of energy and the energy never leaves and so some words are certainly much more powerful than other words. They do have a magnetic force that is part of the human experience, being surrounded by these energy streams as you described it, as you have read in other books and you're studying. That is a good understanding of the way that it works. It creates a powerful draw to certain trains of thought or speaking certain groupings of words that carry with it great power and great energy. To become aware of that is a very powerful step in the enlightenment process for humans. When you realize how easily it is to be drawn into one of those energetic thought forms of words and then those same words came flying out of your mouth creating and adding to that energetic pull, it is no wonder that humans fall prey to those negative statements time and time again.

There is a vigilance that is needed around the spoken word. We are reminding you of the section of the book, The Four Agreements that speaks of words. That is an incredibly accurate description of the diligence that one needs when one is considering opening one's mouths and yet dear ones, we say this with all love and compassion, very little thought is typically given to what comes out of your mouth. The spoken word is one of the most powerful creative tools that you have. The words that come out of your mouth when backed up with intention can become manifest.

You are asking what you need to know about the throat chakra. The throat chakra is the gateway for truth. I Angel Celestina, am the angel of truth in the spoken word. It is through me that you can access these higher truths and are able to bring it through as you are doing now Kelly, I am the Angel of upliftment, I am the angel that edifies.When you were given, as humans, the ability to speak, unlike any other creature on your planet, it came with it an incredible responsibility. The responsibility has gone awry, many humans have lost their ability to discern the spoken word. The creative ability of the spoken word is not really understood by humans. They are beginning to have a grasp of the law of attraction, but they don't realize that every word matters. We do not say this to make you nervous about the words that come out of your mouth, but we do say it to reaffirm that your words are powerful and some effort and energy around what you say would be wise.

You have heard it said, that what you put your energy into, is what gets bigger. So, what you talk about certainly is what gets bigger, and yet, people still seem to need to process out loud, you are the queen of that Kelly. It is true that people need to process verbally, with others, to work themselves through a problem. But the trick to that is to detach yourself, as much as possible, from what it is you are discussing. Because the truth of it is, if you are discussing something with much energy and emotion, it is absolutely creating that very thing. We know that is not what you want us to say, but that is the truth.

Let your words be uplifting, let your words reaffirm to the universe what you want out of life. Be empowered to know that you, your voice, is as important as any voice in the universe. We would speak to you about the concept of standing up for the underdog. This is something you have been very much a proponent of since you were just a young child. Standing up for those that couldn't stand up for themselves or wouldn't stand up for themselves. This is feeling a bit discordant to you as we are bringing it into your mind, but let us just talk it through with you. Let us speak of standing up for the underdog. We would remind you Kelly, that what you resist persists. We are reminding you of the kids you used to stand up for on the school bus when you were young. The energy of welcoming the student into your seat, with kindness and compassion, is a much more productive method than going head-to-head with the bully who was harassing them, and refusing to move over and let them sit down. That is true in all situations. Let the energy of love and compassion flow, but resist the impulse to berate or chastise someone else's behavior, as that is going to create the negative energy.

Avoid justification, everyone can have their own take on any given situation. The energy that is put into justifying oneself is wasted, validation is a much more effective method. Validating how strongly someone else feels about something and perhaps having compassion that they are dealing with those feelings, is much more effective than trying to justify why you might have done or said what you did. Remember not to judge yourself too harshly. This is one of the greatest challenges that humans face. You are the only creature on the planet who has the power of the spoken word, yet every creature has the power of creation, you have the creative ability of the spoken word, which is immense, so try to use it wisely. When you are entering into a potential altercation, if you can allow Angel Gabriel to remind you to shift into that third eye perspective it will be far easier for you to control what comes out of your mouth. When your energy is cleaned, and your chakras are balanced, and you are holding the perspective of the third eye, you will find it much easier to be aware of the words that come out of your mouth. You are seeing how this all works together for the highest good of the individual.

To sum up, it is wise when one speaks to consider the energetic signature of the words. To consider what's going to be spoken. There is so much banter, shall we say, between humans and that is habitual and has no real intent behind it, but it still has power to it. So, we would encourage you to use less words as often as possible. We understand that it will be a difficult thing for one such as yourself to do, as you have this gregarious personality that makes you the life of the party. It is part of your path to awakening Kelly, to be joyful and joyous without having to put words to it. To be more aware of the dialogue that comes out of your mouth at any given time, to observe situations through your third eye which shifts you into that 5th dimension perspective, which takes away much of the need to speak. To not stand up for the downtrodden, to engage with them perhaps offering compassion and upliftment and to just ignore the one who is bringing the negative comments. That is far more productive, to use validation instead of justification in communication. Justification falls on deaf ears, validation will change the energetic signature of the conversation, this will require practice Kelly. Utilizing the daily practices that the angels of the chakras system are laying out will create an environment that is conducive to utilizing your voice in a more productive way. The daily practice so far is the clearing of the energies from your energy field, balancing your chakras, focusing through the third eye, and monitoring the words that you speak.

Color-blue

Body parts-entire throat region, thyroid, neck and shoulders.

Angel Faith

I am Angel faith, the angel of the heart chakra. No greater point is in the human, then that point within the heart space. There are those above and those below we are the representation of the center. You will find it remarkable to tune into the space within your heart and allow the words to come from there. Angel faith, the angel of the heart space. As has been spoken before, we all work together. You are beginning to get a feel for that in your morning time, as you are bringing yourself back to center. You feel the beautiful flow of energy, as we all join in as one, knowing that those to come after me are right here working as well. You are doing well dear one, just step back and allow us to speak. How does the human remain heart centered in a world so full of distraction and annoyances and things that trigger the emotions? Remembering that the human is the species given the experience of emotions. When the chakra system was given, it was with the intent that it would help to facilitate the human to manage their emotional response. There is the emotion of anger, let's say, what is anger? Anger is a physiological response, however, when we speak of love, love is different. It is going to be beyond your understanding, but love exists. Love exists in the very fabric of the universe. We understand that the word is representative of many things on your planet. When we speak of love we speak of that point, yes it would be fine to use the word, zero point, there is a zero point of emotion where it all originates from. The zero point of emotion, is the true emotion, which is love. You ask about the different emotions and what they are and why do we have them. They are created by the human and utilized by the ego, to maneuver the human in whichever direction, and for the most part, will take them away from their true authentic self, which is love.

Emotions are a physiological response, Kelly. When the human body experiences things, there is a mechanism within you, that triggers different chemicals and hormones and endorphins and such, that pours into the bloodstream and gives a physiological response, to whatever is happening. You have given those responses names, anger, joy, happiness, despair, sadness, all of those things are physiological responses to external stimuli. You are asking if love is not, love is a stand-alone experience. There needs to be nothing present to create love, love is its own vibration. There are those human aspects that you have given it, passion, fondness for another human, a baby or a pet or whatever in your experience. You have given that very small branch of the large tree of love the name. That is not the love that resides in your heart center

111

Kelly. The love that resides in the heart center, is the love that surpasses all understanding. It is the love for humanity. It is the love for all non-physical and physical beings. It goes throughout the cosmos. It is the value of just being. It is the value of beingness, it is the value of existence, you can find that connection and it facilitates the oneness of all. It is that deep connectedness, that comes from your heart center and radiates in all directions, connecting you to all that is.

You are thinking of Angel Ariel. Angel Ariel is the angel of oneness. We are the love within that oneness. It is difficult for you to understand that it is all instantaneous. We are coming to you individually to give you a broader understanding, but the love that radiates out from the human, from the heart center, is the glue so to speak, it is the magnetizing force, that connects all. You are aware that the human race was given the experience of emotions. There are not many in the cosmos that have that experience. But all have this love that I speak of. All have that ability to drop into their heart center and feel the brother and sister, those are human terms, but gives you the idea of what we speak. Oneness with the brother and sister, the family, oneness with Mother Earth, with the cosmos, with all of life, that is the purpose of life.. Yes, it radiates out from your heart center like a beacon from a tower. It goes out in all directions, with wonderful healing energy, powerful energy.

It will touch people, when you sit in that space and bring an individual to mind, you are bathing that individual with the frequency of love. That is a very tangible thing you can do, as a human, that many do not know how to take advantage of. You are thinking about prayer and how when you prayed as a young Christian girl , you felt love in your heart. That facilitated the prayers, that is exactly how it works. The frequency of love that you felt for your Jesus and your God, the prayer carried the frequency to them, that is exactly how prayer works. We are giving you an even more expedited method. You can drop into your heart center and speak the name Angel Faith, feel that energy, feel that energetic signal. The energetic signal goes out from your heart, for example as you are picturing your grandson, as he goes for his surgery for his ears, and you picture the love in your heart, not the love for the baby, but the love that is the love of all. You picture that and you let that radiate out and you know that you are affecting that little one as he lays on the table.

You're asking how you remember; how does the human remember to bring these aspects that we are teaching you into your day-

*to-day life. The heart center is an antenna so to speak. Think of how often in the run of a day something quickens your heart, you experience an emotional response. You get that heart centered feeling; become aware of that Kelly, you hear of something that is distressing. You are feeling, right now, like it is your mind, but that is not where the feeling arises. The feeling arises in your heart. Now that you think about it, it makes sense does it not. So, when you have an emotional response to something **that** can remind you to call in the angels, we never leave dear ones, we are always here, but for you to evoke our power consciously and deliberately with intention, it is like turning up the dial so to speak.*

You are asking if we have anything else to tell you about the heart center. It is the point of the energy exchange, Kelly. It is the point of connection within the crystalline grid. It is the point where the energy travels from the center of Mother Earth, up and combines with the cosmic energy that is flowing from the cosmos. That is the best way for us to help you understand it. The point of the heart, the heart center, is where the human is connected to that flow of energy and where you have the ability with your intention to add energy to that flow. Raising the frequency of your planet, that is going back to the beginning, the purpose of this teaching, the purpose of you writing this book. To turn the frequency up, so that the rising tide of frequency will raise all the boats, including those who are living their lives in total ignorance, no judgement, just an observation. The work that you and those who are reading this book and applying the principles within it, can do, is immense! You, and many like you, often get caught in your day Kelly, and judge yourself for living your life and forgetting. But the intentionality that you bring into a moment, even a single moment or several moments in a week, is more than many humans do in a lifetime. You are living more and more consciously, as you progress through your learning. Do not judge yourself Kelly. We do not judge any who are not on the awakened path. But those who are, have great power, have great effect, have great impact, on the whole world as you, with your intentions and your consciousness, do these things to raise your vibrational frequency.

You were born to this earth, but your memory was wiped clean. But the DNA is there. Your journey on this earth over and over, time and time again, is to remember who you are and the power that you hold within you. When you consciously connect, it is like plugging in the toaster. The toaster is fine by itself, but it is so much more functional when it is connected into that power grid. That is exactly as it is for the human. Consciously, through your heart center, connect to that grid of energy, that is the frequency of your planet, the crystalline grid, that travels deep within Mother Earth and completely out to Infinity and back to Infinity within Mother Earth, circulating and flowing that energy. (at this point they are showing me something that looks like an atom, with electrons around it, cycling out to the cosmos, back through the chakras then down to the center of Mother Earth, and continuing out and back, in all directions…)*When you add to that energy with your intention, consciously, it is magnified exponentially. Those who sit in their prayers as you did as a child, add to the grid. Absolutely <u>any</u> act of faith or love or kindness or compassion, adds to the grid. There are wonderful things going on, all around your planet. Many acts of love and kindness, that come out of a sincere motivation. When those things take place, it is absolutely adding to that which we speak of. And it is turning up the frequency of our planet, do not for a moment think, that the only path is through this awakened way. It is not, as you have been shown many times, there is **no** wrong path.*

Let us speak of those who are on the path that is not awakened, who are doing the atrocities and those experiencing the atrocities. There is benefit to the grid in that as well. This is a difficult thing for you to understand, Kelly. But the one who is hurt, if they can find their way to compassion or forgiveness in the light of the atrocity, even without their intention or knowing, that is a great addition to the signature of your planet. That is why there are those who come forward, we know this is a difficult thing for you Kelly, but it is a truth that you need to understand, to live separated from their higher self. When the soul comes forward into the situation that they know has the potential to create the atrocity, they do it with great love.(meaning being born into an abusive family, or mental illness or whatever that would increase the likley hood of them not being able to connect with their higher self) *And then like everyone at birth, they have forgotten their true essence, their true identity so to speak. Their life situations create in them the discordance and the separateness, from their higher self, to create the atrocity or the horrific experience. There are those who come forward and commit the atrocities, and are able to bring themselves back to their higher knowing, within the same incarnation. This does not happen often, and it is very, very difficult for that one, because of the judgments that the world will aim at them. It makes it much more difficult for them to find their way back to the higher frequency, that **is** who they truly are.*

So the work that the enlightened one can do, when you see that one who was the committer of the crime and they are trying to make amends or move forward in the world, we understand that there are those who will bring forward deception and deceit, but there is the occasional one who has their feet on the path to knowing who they really are again, see all with compassion. The biggest point in this, is that you have the choice to add to the judgment, to add to the negative energy, the negative frequency on your planet or you have the ability to add to the frequency of love and compassion, which raises the energy, and raises the vibration of the crystalline grid. It is stepping away from the vibration of judgment dear one. Judgment of other people's actions as right and wrong, this we know is incredibly hard. You struggle with your kids and what they do and find yourself judging their actions, this is a very small example of what goes on, all the time, on your planet. Every single experience is brought up for judgment. Every single experience, every nuance of life is pulled up and looked at and judged as either good or bad. The more that this is done, the more that the frequency of your planet will continue to be where it is. Use the energy of the chakra system to come all together through the knowing, through the balance and the correct openness. Through the third eye, through truth and coming into your heart and observe, simply observe, without judgment, of good or bad or right or wrong, seeing without judgment. (She is speaking of all the angles up to this point) *This is the energy that you seek dear one. This is the energy of knowing, of love, compassion, all that we, in the non-physical realm, are pulling you towards.*

You're asking how you live in your day-to-day life and let go of judgments. You have been consciously aware of needing this and you continue to struggle because of the human condition, Kelly. It is that signature of the human, it is that energetic pull that you have. Yes, the ego plays in this, the ego is whispering in your mind making you decide if something is good or bad. But remember things just <u>are</u>. If you can adopt that, as often as possible, celebrating... not really celebrating, in a sense celebration is a judgment as well, it is a judgment of good, this is getting into a much deeper level of understanding, Kelly. Something that is very, very difficult for people to understand. There can be a deep sense of love within any situation. It does not come from external circumstances. When the human can find that neutral position, with that deep sense of love, they are much less susceptible to the pulling and pushing and the ups and the downs. Even as we say this, your mind goes to joy and happiness and fun and all the things that humans enjoy. Yes, that is absolutely true, but when your emotions are able to be pulled in that direction, which is a human direction, they are also able to be pulled in the other direction, then the wave of despair and the wave of grief or anger can grab you. This is an incredibly difficult concept for the human to grasp. We are not saying we do not want you enjoying the higher end of the emotional scale. We are saying there is an emotional, vibrational, swing that can happen.

You were asking if that means we do not want you to be joyous. That is not what we are saying. This is but another layer of understanding for you. There is deep joy in that place of neutrality and knowing. There is deep, deep love and happiness and gratitude in that place of neutrality. You are looking at the thing <u>outside</u> of you that causes emotions, that is what we are drawing your attention to, yes you are beginning to understand... There can be all those high emotions, regardless of the circumstances. Being at the whim of these circumstances is what we are talking to you about. When you can feel the joy and the love and the fun that happens from that point, that center point in your heart. When the emotion bubbles up from that connection, to <u>all that is,</u> there is unlimited joy and love and wonder that you are connected to. That is that point within, that everyone always speaks of. "Look within" they say, "look within" that is what they are speaking of.

There is always access to that greater knowing, that greater joy. That is the heart space, dear one, that is your connection. We are not saying that there is not the enjoyment of external things, but when you are living your life in that place of ultimate joy and love and happiness and fun you don't need them. Then the "experience" or "observation" happens, it's not the observation that is causing the joy and the wonder, if you can understand what we are trying to say to you. When that is the case, you are going to be far less vulnerable to the things that are coming up in your life, the annoyances and the experiences. When you are not looking at your external world, you are looking at your internal world, that is the heart chakra dear one, that is the heart chakra.

You're asking if there is a practice for the human to do. That is good, let us speak about that. You do your work that you have learned up to this point. You complete through the last three chakras and then you come into your heart space, you breathe into that heart space. You breathe the knowing of the joy, the knowing of the love, the knowing of the happiness, and compassion that is there. Not even needing to think of any circumstance that will raise your vibration. Knowing you are connected to all circumstances, across all dimensions and all timelines, gives you that joy. You are connected to <u>every</u> joyful moment that you have ever experienced, or ever <u>will</u> experience, across all timelines, *across all dimensions, across all realms and in all circumstances and in all incarnations. You are connected to every joyful, happy, fun moment that has ever gone or will go. Feel what that feels like in your heart, feel your vibration rise and stream out from you into the grid, as you experience everything that has ever happened. Whatever is going on outside of you in this physical incarnation, matters absolutely not. You are connected to the greatness, you are connected to the glory, you are connected to the sovereignty of all timelines, all dimensions, all experiences, that have ever gone before. That energy is coming to you, through your heart center, and it is going from you to that heart center ... you are so very loved.*

Color-green

Body parts-lungs, heart, arms, and hands

Angel Cassiel

Help me to feel your energy, Angel Cassiel, help me to be a clear vessel, help me to open and get out of the way.

Step back dear one, allow for me to come through with the message for you this day. Step back dear one let us speak. The angels of the chakra system, the angels of the chakra system, it has been some days since we have been together in this way (It had been the holidays and I hadn't written or meditated much) *I have been patiently waiting my turn(laughs) for I have a message for you and your book. Step back dear one, step back and allow the words to come. Allow the words to come easily and flow, speaking the name of Angel Cassiel as we come through with the message of the third chakra. Moving down the energy body from those above and those in center now you begin into those that are connecting you more strongly to Mother Earth.*

I am Angel Cassiel; I am the angel of the third chakra. I am between those grounding energies and your heart. I am the next step in the energy development. You have very little knowledge of this chakra. It makes you uneasy as you come into this meditation, for you know that whatever we bring through will be completely from us, which is always the way that it is. We enjoyed watching you read this morning, as you read a chapter or two of the other angels and were overwhelmed by the message, knowing there would be no way, even with what prior knowledge you had of that particular chakra, that you would be able to bring through that message. Dear one, that is as it is today. You will allow me to bring through what we would have the human know, as we bring the connection between the frequency of the lower self, the self that is in the denser vibration, carrying around the human body, that connection between that human self and all that there is, all the connection to Source Energy. Creating that bridge that we spoke of in the very beginning of your book. Yes, dear ones we have been helping you along in your life from the time you were born.

There is a great deal that the solar plexus holds. It holds many knowings and is the gateway to healing. This is the center of healing the wounds that hold the human from being able to merge and connect with their higher self. We are the angel of the esoteric human/spirit healing. We search your mind for the word that represents what we are trying to say, it is the healings that must happen, the damage that happens to the human, that affects the connection between the spiritual self and the personality. That which you incarnated into and have lived, life experiences, many of those are held in the area of the solar plexus. It is the area of healing, the area of merging the energy of Mother Earth, that you have only recently learned about, your beautiful, blessed, relationship and communion with her, with the energy of the higher chakras. We are showing you in your mind, the visual that we gave you, yes dear ones your angels and your guides work together, so yes, we can say that we gave you the download that showed the surface of the earth, so to speak being at the heart center. (They are describing a download they gave me several months ago and have been teaching me about ever since. They showed me the human embedded in the energy of Mother Earth up to the heart chakra. That the lower chakras resonate with the energy of Mother Earth and the upper chakras resonate with the energy of the cosmos. It is at the heart that they meet). *It's a figurative thing of course, we are talking about the energy body. The lower chakras, the earth-tone chakras, are the chakras that reach into Mother Earth and hold you with that infinite, as we have shown you, that infinite space within the center of Mother Earth, that we have shown you on your journey. These chakras, the third chakra and those below... You noticed the fourth one below your heart, and just as there is Angel Ariel, there is the fourth connection below. You have been a bit confused by that over the last several days, since you read that list and realized that there was an extra chakra, an extra angel for the chakra system. That will unfold for you beautifully when it is time.* (They have counted down from eight, but there are nine angels that were in the book they directed me to. I have no idea about the role of the last one we will just have to wait and see!)

As you take a sip of your tea and you swallow it into your system, you feel the warmth go down into your body. That is a representation of the way the solar plexus, this chakra, the yellow chakra, the chakra that vibrates with the frequency of yellow can interact with your body. We create the sips of the energy of that beautiful root system that goes deep within Mother Earth, and we alchemize the energy to be utilized by the upper chakras to change the frequency as it comes up through the chakra system. I am the last in line and I create the healing ability of the energy as it merges with the energy of the upper chakras. When you are asking for a healing dear one, put your energy into the solar plexus, you have had very little experience with these energy fields. It has not been your go to, so to speak. But this has been established throughout your journey, every person born, every human is born with an affinity, let us say, for either the upper half or the lower half of the chakra system. Remember dear one we are one system; we are showing you this for the sake of understanding. When you complete your journey through these energy systems that we have laid out for you, you will have the ability to utilize it as a single unit. But let us go into the specifics of the third chakra.

It is the sounding ground, shall we say, for the energy of Mother Earth to come up through your grounding system and spend time as is necessary for the individual, for the healing energy that comes from Mother Earth to be able to be utilized to the maximum ability by the human. There are times when the human needs big waves of denser, that is not quite right, we gave you previously a visual of the frequency of the lower half, not lower in the human understanding of darkness or not good, those are all human judgment and human words and terms but you are getting what we are trying to say to you, we showed you the continuum of frequencies that go out in both directions, to all dimensions and all timelines, all realms and all incarnations, yes dear ones this is important.

Narration- this is very complex and convoluted so I want to take a minute to explain. Several months ago, I received a download. As I have explained before they have begun to give me many pictures, and knowings. Sometimes it is very difficult to put those things into words. What they showed me in that download was the human body basically engulfed within Mother Earth up to the heart space. They were showing me the heart space being the place of merging, merging the energy of the lower chakras with the energy of the higher chakras. The representation being that the higher chakras are connected with the energy of the cosmos, and the lower chakras are connected to the energy of Mother Earth. During this download they showed me infinite space within the center of Mother Earth. And they refer to it as infinite all the time. At that time, they described to me a continuum of frequency. The continuum goes forever to higher frequencies and forever on the other end to lower frequencies. They explained to me that there is a great amount of understanding and knowledge within the lower end of that continuum but that humans, when they think the word lower, associate it with less than... or bad. But that is not the case. When they give me information and pictures it must come through the filters of my own mind. At that time, I saw the continuum on a horizontal axis. When I used to teach my CNA class, I often used the term continuum for a variety of things so that was a familiar visual for me. But I always visualized it horizontally.

As the energies from that part of the continuum that you, with your human mind, see on the horizontal axis. We are showing you now that it is a vertical access. Yes, my dear, feel the energy turn up with that knowing. Sit for a moment and feel that vertical axis of energy that goes to Infinity in the center of Mother Earth into the energetic planes and dimensions and goes to Infinity to the cosmos. You are very familiar with the frequencies of the heart chakra and above. We are introducing you to the solar plexus chakra, the yellow chakra and below. Feel that frequency Kelly. Breathe into the solar plexus... Utilizing the yellow color... (I took several breaths) *the colors are used for access. Because you, in this incarnation, have always resonated with the chakra system from your heart and above, the colors were not needed. We told you early in the angelic downloads to not discount the other tools that come with the chakra system. Now, we want to bring into the knowingness the colors. We would ask you dear one, to go back and introduce the color into each chapter of your book explaining that Angel Cassiel asked you to do this. This is very much part of healing.*

When you utilize the colors of the chakra system it takes on a very subtle difference in frequency. Each of the chakras do, it is a doorway that lets the beautiful breeze in to the particular chakra. A breeze of healing energy as well. You have also been introduced in a very rudimentary way to the body systems that are also associated with each chakra system and this too, I ask you to introduce and explain in each chapter of your book. Utilize your Internet for the specificness of that information. It is not always necessary dear one, to reinvent the wheel. This information has come through to many, in many ways.

I Angel Cassiel, am the angel that facilitates utilizing the chakra system for healing. I bring the energies together, that is not exactly right Kelly. I alchemize the energies and the frequencies on this end of the energetic continuum of vibration and frequency. I alchemize it to blend with the heart center and the energies of the higher realms as they move into the heart center for the perfection of the blending. Because the heart center is love and so attuned to love there was no need to have the alchemizing station of the higher end as it entered the heart center. This is a very simplistic explanation dear one, but it is enough for us, for today.

So yes, Angel Cassiel is the angel of alchemy. When you breathe your energy into any of the chakras along the chakra system above, it is I who alchemize the vibrations that do not serve the human at the present time and send them through the chakra system down into our beautiful Mother Earth. I am that which assist the alchemy within the body. There is great power here, for that one who has learned to thoroughly alchemize energy. It is a great part of this, you have been using the word hack that we are giving you, it is not a shortcut dear one, it is what the human race, who are vibrating at such a higher understanding, need at this time.

You know that your planet is undergoing an amazing transformation. Utilizing the energy systems of your body in a more efficient way, because you are vibrating so intensely, with a much greater ability for understanding and remembering who you are. It is part of your understanding of that continuum of frequency that we are helping you to come to a greater place of knowing about. The yellow energy system, the third chakra, Angel Cassiel Angel Cassiel, it is an unusual name, you will become more familiar with it and more comfortable. We are the point on that continuum of alchemy. We bring the energy, yes dear one, we show you that beautiful loop of the crystalline pathway that we have been showing you, to the level of understanding, that you are able to absorb, at this time period. It is a very good and functional understanding. But do know dear one, there will be layers and layers of understanding that will come in addition to this.

We are showing you that beautiful loop, and how the energy, as it cycles into Mother Earth, and it comes up into the human, through Angel Cassiel, through the yellow chakra, being alchemized for the greatest good of the human who is bringing it in. Then it merges in that beautiful heart center the beautiful green heart center. Then it goes up, up through the throat, up through the third eye and up through the crown, being guided by and drawn forth by Angel Ariel into the beautiful purification, the oneness of the white light and it passes through her into the cosmos to get threads of information, threads of knowing, threads of DNA. This is a lot for you dear one, but the energy carries the frequency of all of these things as it cycles and comes back to the point on the grid, on the web, the point on the web that is your heart center. It merges, it comes into my center, and it is alchemized to do whatever needs to be done. It may need to be stored for a later time. It may need to be sent to Mother Earth, to either wait within Mother Earth or wait within any of the other centers below me in the continuum. And it loops into Mother Earth picking up and releasing as is necessary to come forth into the point of your solar plexus. Where a merging can take place, an alchemizing can take place, for the healing of the human, for whatever is necessary to heal at this time.

You ask if this is where the healing for the physical body comes and yes, it is the place where the alchemizing of the energy, as it is sent into the different points along the chakra system, we are showing you the colors of the chakra system, and that the chakra system resonates with a body system. So that chakra will bring, to whichever place in the cycle that it is, will bring the knowings and the imbalances and impurities that might be dwelling within that body system and it is within this cycle of your energy flowing that balance can happen. Describe what you are seeing Kelly, (it's hard to explain it's almost like they are showing the salt and the pepper that would go into a recipe for this particular healing whatever is out in the cosmic realm that is needed is collected on the cycle and then brought down. There is an adding to, and taking away from, that is happening) *down through the vertical chakra system into and through the heart and into the solar plexus where it is alchemized, changed into whatever is the highest that the human can absorb at this time. It's changed to a degree... then it is sent into the infiniteness that is Mother Earth to do the same thing, cycling and bringing, releasing and bringing back what is needed for this particular healing to occur. This is going on all the time Kelly, all of the time.*

Narration-this information is very convoluted; it is coming through with many pictures. They are showing me the constant flow of energy, up to the cosmos, down into our energy system, through the heart into the third chakra to be alchemized. It seems at this point that Angel Cassiel assesses the energy and alchemizes it for our highest good. Then sending it into the loop, that goes into Mother Earth, carrying with it anything that is no longer needed by the individual. As it cycles through Mother Earth, it also picks up frequencies that cycle back to the human again to be alchemized within the third chakra, taking with it what is needed, into the cosmos and what cannot be used by the human.

You ask why then, are healings difficult, and we would say to you, they are not. There is great strength in the human understanding the ability of the chakra system, to go within and bring the discordance out into this flow of energy. When the human can ask, with intention and believe in the possibility, then the healing can occur. We know dear one, this is an area that you struggle with. We know you believe in miracles and healing for others, but it is difficult for you to believe for yourself. So, at this time dear one, let us just leave it at this and you can begin to know that we are Angel Cassiel, and we bring the healing. We are alchemizing, storing and changing and putting into the cycle, the call for what is needed, either above or below and drawing it into this point of the alchemizing station for the human. That is right dear one, it is more than healing for the body, it is the healing for the many aspects of your soul and personality in this incarnation.

You ask dear one why you suffer with pain in your human body. It is because of the self-imposed limitations and conflict that you have always carried within your energy. The battle you have raged within, between the frequencies of understanding and the frequency of limitation... You are beginning to wrap your mind around the magnificence that is you. The magnificence that is every single human. Because you are God on earth, you are an extension, you are part of, you are one with All, including God. You have dear ones, struggled greatly with the thought of that.

Narration-she directed me to go into meditation, so I did... Now I'm asking her if there's anything more, she wants to tell me about the 3rd chakra.

It is in this third chakra, where the human's inability to trust their own voice, their own inner knowing, causes disruption. You ask if there is a process to develop that trust. It will come in the practicing of the flowing of energy as you feel the changes that will take place in you more consciously now, more deliberately now, turning up the energy now. As this energy cycles it can create within you the frequency of the highest that you are bringing to you on this timeline. The healing of the inner child, the many aspects of the inner child, is done within and through this chakra. You will see much of the wounding that takes place of the human, is held within these vibrational frequencies of these lower chakras. you will understand dear one, this is enough for now. Except we would say know how completely you can trust this; you can trust the energy to bring to you and take from you what it needs to. You can trust yourself to remember often. You can trust yourself to utilize this energy system for all the things that it represents. You can trust Kelly, and all humans can trust as well.

Color-yellow

Body parts-digestive system, pancreas, and muscles.

Angel Daniel

Angel Daniel, the Angel of the second chakra, the Angel who resonates with orange. What would you have us know about the second chakra?

We are ready to come through, the question dear one, is are you ready to allow us? That is the question! We are Angel Daniel, we have been with you all of your life. We have tapped upon your shoulder at different times trying to get your attention. This has been quite an undertaking. Trying to disseminate and digest the angels of the chakra system. There is much that we do to assist the human, on their journey on planet earth. We are your connection; we work as a unit. We are the connection between Mother Earth and the cosmos. We are the vibrational frequencies that allow the human to manage their emotional system, their emotional body. The emotional body is what we, Angel Daniel, have the greatest connection to. We are that gut feeling that humans speak of so often, that emotional knowing. The collectiveness at the human level. The collection of all that has gone before and all that will come, rests within this chakra. The chakra that resonates with orange. It is the gut feeling that rests here. Breathe the color orange, fill your aura with orange.

You have far less prior knowledge and understanding of the lower chakras than you did the higher chakras. You have lived your life very much connected to the cosmos, and as you have learned up to this point, that is through the top half of the chakra system. But the bottom half of the chakra system is your relationship with Mother Earth. That is a much newer vibration for you, you have always loved the earth, in your way, but did not truly understand that she is your mother, and holds you in her arms of love and comfort. She is always there helping you, helping as the energy cycles down through her and she works with the energy to give it what you are the closest vibrational match to. Then she takes out what is not a match for you, taking out of the trash is not exactly accurate, it is more the vibrational matching, the frequency matching, of what you would be able to utilize, is a much closer explanation of what Mother Earth does for this energy cycle. There is no trash, there is just energy that is not a close enough vibrational match for it to be utilized for the individual human.

We are Angel Daniel; we are your gut instincts. We are the birthing place of your intuition. Again, we show you your third eye and the discernment that comes with Angel Gabriel. Remembering this is all an instantaneous collaboration that takes place. You are understanding the different threads, the different colors of the rainbow, as it cycles throughout your body system. Angel Daniel gives that gut hit when you know to not go this way or that. Yes, of course Angel Gabriel is helping in the process, so are all the angels. It is the holding of the knowledge, the holding of the life experiences, even across many dimensions and many realms and many lifetimes and paths that you have traveled. This is where you find your access to that point of your energetic knowing. You have always had a very good understanding of how your intuition works. You explained it to your students many times, utilizing the example of a computer and if you do not overthink things, all of the knowledge stored within the computer will tally up, so to speak, or make an assessment, is another way to say it, to give you that nudge to go either left or right in any given situation. Those knowings are stored within this chakra.

As the energy circulates through Mother Earth up through the cosmos and down through your energy system, we are adding to it the knowledge from past experiences, the aspects that you carry that will help you in your discernment. It is much more common for humans to be, or it was in the past, it is getting less common now, for humans to be more closely associated with their lower chakra system, than the higher aspects of the chakra system. That is changing with time, again, not a hierarchy, just a level of understanding, of your environment and living within this world. It is important for the chakra system to be balanced, for the human to have the greatest access to the powers that they possess.

An awakening, a connection to this energy with deliberate intent, is needed to develop that balance. Many people have experiences throughout their lives of a sexual or base nature. Humans were originally designed in that way, this part of your nature was given and intended to facilitate the species in many different ways. Yes, of course, with procreation and the population of your planet. We are showing you, in your mind, the many aspects of human sexuality. There has been a tremendous imbalance, over the previous decades in the human, as this part of your human ego, developed into a much bigger, broader aspect than was intended. An awareness came quickly to the human, in the early part of their evolution, that a great deal of power could be wielded from this point, this base sexuality point. Because of this, humans tend to carry a great deal of pain in this charka. It is a point in the human collective that needs great healing and balance. It is a difficult thing for you, we are giving you much knowing with pictures and downloads within your mind and it's hard for you to put into words. If you can remind yourself of what we have given you before, there is no wrong, there are just experiences on this earth. The things that you see through your human eyes, as atrocities, we view as no more than an experience in time. Remembering that time does not exist. So, the suffering that you think goes on for long periods, really from our perspective, is very fleeting. But it is a catalyst, it is something that has been used within the human to advance their evolution. The wielding of this power, the power to hold with such intimacy and adoration and care or the power to debase and humiliate and hurt, within a given moment in time. You are struggling to wrap your mind around if this was an intended thing or if this evolved. Your understanding of it evolves, knowing the potential was always there. Every human is born with all on the continuum, all the infinite possibilities and choices and they make these choices. Yes, dear one, understanding that some of the choices are made in the non-physical before you come forth. Choices that increase the likelihood of the base actions, the one born to the mentally ill person for example. It is such a difficult thing for you to understand, how much of this is agreed upon in love and support in non-physical, for the evolution and evolvement of your humanity.

Narration-this concept is difficult and very important for us to understand. Decisions that are made between souls before they come to the earth are agreed upon in love. One agrees to be born into the family that abuses drugs and alcohol, or has mental illness, with the knowing that the likelihood of terrible things happening to them is great. They know that this can create in them the imbalance that will allow them to do the awful actions as well. They do this through love.

We bring you back dear one to us, Angel Daniel, and the second charka. This is the storage place of much of the human pain and suffering that happens to humans throughout their incarnations. But remember, that with knowledge there is power. Knowing that a deep conscious dive into this chakra can unlock and release much of the pain and heal much of the scars across all dimensions, across all timelines, across all realms and all experiences. That when you dive, we are showing you the deep vastness of orange color that you can evoke consciously as you go into your meditation, asking Angel Daniel to help you to excavate the pains of other lifetimes, other incarnations, that are brought forward from lifetime to lifetime to be healed. As the human collective raises its vibrational signature, a greater depth of healing must occur.

So, we would ask you to go into meditation activating your entire chakra system, including those that will come after us. Asking for the help of Mother Earth and her support and her energy as you delve into this. We are showing you a library, an akashic record, as you say that, you do not know if you are using it correctly, but there is akash stored within this area. Allow the words and look them up later Kelly there is a great storage of experiences, the energy of the experiences, stored here. It is the frequency of an event, the energy of an event and this event could have happened in any number of incarnations even any number of races, realms, dimensions, all this fits. It will require a deep opening into this library, this akashic record, of these kinds of energies that need to be healed.

You are asking why humans took something that could be so beautiful, the coupling between two people in love and allowed it to become this often-horrific act of violence. It is the Yin and the Yang, Kelly; we know this is very uncomfortable for you dear girl. We know that this is making you uncomfortable as you are thinking of those who have been abused. But it is what we would have you know at this time. It is the nature of duality, that the perfection of anything cannot be known without distortion. There is an energy to this, a language to this sexual energy. There is a knowing, a beingness of understanding within this, that we want to bring forth for you at this time. The greatest heights can only be achieved when the greatest depths are available as well. The human has come forth navigating these highs and lows so to speak, the Yin and the Yang energy. You have had many incarnations and you have experienced all aspects of all these things, in many lifetimes, in a very in-deliberate, unconscious way. But that does not take the knowingness of the whole, the knowing is stored within this akash, this chakra is the doorway to that. So much is represented within this chakra system. The whole broadband of...

Narration-I am struggling at this point in the download, there is so much information coming through and it is so difficult to wrap my mind around all of it. I'm struggling physically as well as emotionally. They have me place my two pointer fingers together on my third eye and my thumbs each extended down to my jaw with my other three fingers together. They had never done that before. But it seemed to have a calming effect on me.

There are aspects of the human that are specific to humans. We spoke to you in the beginning that the chakra system was given to you as *a tool to handle and navigate your emotional experiences, your emotional body within this dimension. This continuum of, the word sexuality is not correct, it is only a small part of it, baseness, of humans with the opposite as well, is stored within this chakra. It is how you have access between incarnations, when you learn that you can reach into these prior knowings. For the human to be able to find there... (holy **** this is hard to understand!)*

The continuum of the base part of the human condition, finding a way to love, with the urgings that come from this aspect of being human. Remembering that we have no judgments, these are experiences. We are feeling your frustration, you again are talking of the petri dish, we do not view it that way Kelly. You are not only an experiment in a petri dish, dear one. You will come to understand, it is all about love, it is about finding your way back to love. Filling this part of the chakra system with love. This is difficult for you at this time, but you are doing fine Kelly.

You are asking for us to sum up what we would have you put into your book about the second chakra. The chakra that resonates with orange. You ask if the chakra system is working on someone who is completely un-evolved, of course it is! You are very twirled up with this, as we knew this would be difficult for you. That is why we gave you such a beautiful download earlier this morning, helping you to know that you are on the right path. It is understandable, dear one, that you would find this confusing. We would say let this be a two-part download, transcribe and make sense of what we have given you. Utilizing the pictures in your mind and adding, as you need to, for understanding. Once you have done that then let us come to you once again with the remainder of the download that we would have for you.

Do not feel that this is not successful Kelly. Do not judge it. That is the ego, you must take the information that we are giving you at any given time and utilize it to the best of your ability. Building one upon the other, one knowing upon the next. You are so very loved, and your angels are supporting you. Do not feel that there is a negative thing that has come to you during this, it has not, it is an understanding. The base nature of humans, this is not news to you, we are just giving you the foundational understanding, the energetic understanding behind it. So that the human who reads your book will be able to decipher and go into this point of their energy system and do the healings that can affect across all dimensions and all timelines...

Narration-I let some time go by for my energy and emotions to settle down. I then felt ready to ask Angel Daniel if there was any more he wanted to share with us.

You have taken some days to reflect upon the information that we have given you. That is a good thing, dear one. You reached out to your friend Jody and read the words to her, needing validation in this matter. This is understandable. It is not surprising when information that is so new to you comes through, that you question. That is the nature of being human. We understand this. We know you had a sense of human guilt, that you questioned. (Guilt because I doubted what came through) *But dear one, that is part of what you bring to the table. The discernment, we would have it no other way. You ask us now if there is more that we would like to bring forth for this section of the book. The way to interact with the second chakra, the chakra that resonates with orange.*

As the angels of the chakras work in unison, there will be great power in the mechanism. We pointed out to you the specifics of the second chakra, as often, humans have many things stored in this area that need to be healed. There would be a specific healing and balancing of this chakra that we would bring forth. Even one such as you, who does not think that there are injuries in that area of your system, remember dear one, we are giving you information that crosses all timelines, all dimensions and all experiences and all realms. So, you can trust us dear one, there is that, in this area, for you as well. You will sit in meditation, and you will go through the processes that we have given you in this section of the book. You will garner your balance in all of the other chakras. Then you will breathe the orange into the area of your abdomen. You will breathe deep within, swirling the orange, like a whirlwind, with the intention of dislodging, loosening, bringing the memories or any pain that is residing in this area out. It will not require specific memories to come up. That may or may not happen. Just go in with the knowing that across all dimensions, there have been these experiences, because as we have spoken before in many different ways, the human that is you, the spirit, the energy that is you, has come forward in many dimensions and realms and in timelines and experiences along the continuum.

Narration-what they are guiding me to understand at this time is something they've said before in different ways, we have incarnated into all aspects of the human condition. That is a difficult thing for me to wrap my mind around, but they are giving it to me in so many different ways that I know it to be the truth. We have been the perpetrator and we have been the victim in all ways.

There is healing that needs to happen for the perpetrator, as well as healing that needs to happen for the victim. Within your akash, there are all of these things. Breathing the color orange into this part of the system, swirling it, invoking the power of the chakra team. All of your guides and all of your angels, asking for their help to go into this area and bring forth that which needs to heal. Across all dimensions, across all timelines. Command the energy and the memories and the scars and the guilt and the trauma and all that has gone before or will ever go, command it to be healed by your angelic team. See the orange energy swirling within you. Seeing the orange coming out, radiating out of your body across all timelines and all dimension and all realms for the highest good. Feeling the energy as it rolls through you and out, into the orange burst around you, shards of orange energy radiating out from this center point carrying with it all that it needs to.

Seeing the energy of the cosmos and the energy of Mother Earth coming together in this point and blending and swirling, round and round like a spiral going around and around, blending and gathering, taking a deep breath within and sending the energy out to be alchemized, down to Mother Earth, that which belongs to Mother Earth, then up to the cosmos, that which belongs to the cosmos. Carrying on this flow of energy, all the pain, all the guilt, all the horror that remains, within all your body cells. Within all the bodies across all the timelines, across all dimensions, across all realms, and frequencies and vibrations. Carrying anything that is not serving the highest good, carrying it away. That which is able to be released at this time, carrying it away, carrying it to Mother Earth, seeing the flow that we've shown you before, seeing the energetic flow, going deep into the earth, going up through the chakras, gathering up what needs to be gathered, going up through the solar plexus being alchemized, up through the heart system, out to the cosmos, down through the top of the head down through the heart center, being alchemized in the solar plexus down and gathering any that is needed to be released within the second chakra, in the abdominal area, down into Mother Earth, picking up and releasing, coming up through to the cosmos, picking up and releasing as it flows.

Let the gratitude and appreciation for this process fill your heart, the love and the knowing that you are so supported in this journey. Anything that needs to be alchemized, anything that resonates with the

*orange frequency, any feelings, any remnants of any upsets or
disappointments or judgments or grief or hurt around this part of your
energetic field, letting it flow until you feel the balance come. You will
know when you are balanced, this may need to be done over time, there
is a time for everything. There are times when there is a purpose for the
carrying of the energy and only that which no longer serves your highest
good will be released. That is to say, that within a future time, there may
be more ready to be released. For this you must trust, dear ones. You ask
if there is more that we would give you, Angel Daniel the angel of the
second chakra that resonates with the orange. Just to know dear ones
how loved you are, to know that we are with you always, and you are
deeply, deeply loved.*

Narration-the second-half of the book has blown my mind! But
this last section has been the most difficult for me so far. If I have learned
anything, on my journey up to this point, it is that humans need to find
their way to trust. To have faith in that which we cannot see or
understand. The process that Angel Daniel described is a further
utilization of that energy flow that they showed me in the very first
several chapters of this book. It has come forward in many different
ways, in many different processes. What I see in my mind when they
describe it, the way that Angel Daniel did, it is difficult to describe but
I'm going to try. It is like an energetic infinity sign or figure eight, with
the point of crossing being our chakra system. Cycling down into Mother
Earth through the body up to the heavens down through the body and
into Mother Earth. Repeating the pattern in all directions, over and over
and over, creating this three-dimensional overlapping, ball of energy. I
believe that we are going to find, as we put this into practice, that it holds
great power. Please remember that you must utilize intention and your
ability to command with passion for these processes to work.

Color- orange

Body parts-genitals, womb, kidney, bladder, circulatory system.

Angel Sarah and Angel Michael

Let the words come dear one, we are Angel Sarah we are the angel of the first chakra, in the human chakra system. The energy points that humans are the most familiar with, the seven major chakras of the spinal chakra system. As you know there are many chakras throughout the body, many different points of energetic resonance that can be used for a number of purposes. I am Angel Sarah, I speak now, I am here to bring through the message that you would have around the first chakra. The chakra that resonates with red, red the color of blood, the color of life.

Step back dear one and let us speak, for we would paint a picture of the utilization of this chakra. The point on the chakra system at the base of the spine. The base of all of the vessels and nerves that run throughout the spinal column. Being the central point in the human body, the connection between the brain and the lower part of the body system. The spinal column branches out to all the body systems. The final point, the base point so to speak, is that point of branching, that goes down through your legs, into your feet, that walk upon Mother Earth. This point, in the flow of the pelvic floor, is the joining point where so many impulses and nerves and vessels go through, but also dear one, where the energy is branching down through the legs to the feet, to connect with Mother Earth. It is part of that beautiful cycling of energy, that cycles through the earth, to the heavens, as we have discussed many times up to this point.

Narration-they are showing me a black hole at the end of this continuum within Mother Earth. I looked up the definition of a black hole and it said,"black holes are regions in space where an enormous amount of mass is packed into a tiny volume" that is a fairly accurate description of what I see in my mind and how they make me feel. They give me the feeling of infinite space... that's the best I can do to describe it.

Humans do not utilize both ends of this continuum as well as they could. The energy of the sacral chakra is a more intense vibration, a more resounding frequency, because it goes into the infinity that is Mother Earth. It is the connection point where the vessels split and go down your legs and innervate your feet and your feet walk upon this earth. It is that connection, because of the intensity or the frequency of this chakra, when it becomes out of balance, it has a more resounding effect on the human. Because of the density of the energy in this area, even a slight disruption or imbalance causes great impact on the entire system.

I am Angel Sarah, I am the Angel of the first chakra, I wave my flag of energy in this area, calling your attention to this part of yourself. The significance of the branching is very pertinent. Humans are an extension of Mother Earth. The human is part of Mother Earth, one with Mother Earth energetically. We have spoken before of this relationship. The chakra system is what facilitates this energetic connection between Mother Earth and the cosmos, with the human, being that central point, that nucleus, that central point. The central point of the chakra system as we have spoken of before, is the heart, where the energy comes from the cosmos and from Mother Earth and combines with the different influences of the other chakra points along the way. This is the understanding that we would have you have. We have been giving you reminders throughout your day lately, we are giving you the picture to help you understand.(They are showing me puffs of breath, of all the different colors along the chakra system, puffing into the center of the body and then out. This has come to me over the last week or so, any time I needed any support. I would breath in this way and I would feel better). *When you breathe in and out of the entire chakra system, and you utilize the colors, there is a balancing and a tending to that happens, that will facilitate the highest good. When you combine all of the work that you do with the chakra system, all of the various processes that we have given you, throughout this section of the book. When you practice those and you have seen that it requires some practice and some study. This work that we have given you, the words that we have given you in this book, are words that need to be committed to memory. It is not going to take a great deal of time, but life has certainly interrupted the flow with the holiday season, and you have not been able to bring this book through as fast as the last one. Do not let that be a judgment Kelly, it is just an observation. That is why you may not be remembering the things that came through from the first angels, that you have not necessarily been practicing.*

We are reiterating to you dear one, that this process is to be utilized as one, as a whole. We will be bringing it all together, but it is something that you, according to the degree of imbalance that you feel, is the amount of time and energy and effort that you'll need to put into the intention and the focus behind utilizing these procedures. But it is all one, when you go back and read, you're going to see that each built upon the other and it very much goes to the breath. This does not surprise you at all Kelly. The breath is the balancing point for the human. The breath is life. So, when you breathe the colors into the chakra system starting with the color at the crown and ending with the color at the root and you see those colors, roy-g-biv, as you learned it in school, the colors of the rainbow.

When you breathe in and you breathe them out and you see the colored puffs go into the atmosphere and then you breathe them in and you breathe them out, and you breathe them in and you breathe them out. Using your intention, focusing on the highest good and asking your angels to assist... there will come a point of balance. When you know there has been enough from these breaths in and out and the vibrational output of the chakra system is in the right vibrational frequency, then you begin to loop out the energy into the figure eight that we have described to you previously. You will visualize the puffs of color and you will continue with your breath, cycling out to the cosmos and to the center of Mother Earth, through the colored puffs of energy, within the human chakra system. Breathe with your intention and your visualization and you will establish a rhythm and the energy will flow. Each color will adjust itself, as it is necessary to adjust. You will feel the energy increase and you will feel the experience throughout your entire body. This is the healing that is happening throughout your body, every cell of your body getting exactly what it needs.

Narration-at this time they are cueing me to breathe and the energy is turning up, As the rhythmic breaths increase, they begin to show me the energy of the chakras, the colors, moving out from my body in all directions creating a rainbow colored bubble, if you will, around my body. I am seeing the energy flowing through that multi-colored sphere of energy as it flows to the cosmos, then down to Mother Earth, and it continues to do that figure eight cycle in all directions.

Seeing the esoteric field expanding out, and out. Seeing it blend with Mother Earth, blending with Mother Earth and blending with the cosmos. Breathing it with your hands utilizing your hands to breathe and pull the energy towards your center and push the energy out with the power of your intention (at this point my hands are doing the heaven and earth movement that I learned from Donna Eden) *visualizing the pulsating in and out, the breathing in and out, of this beautiful, beautiful connected energy. Breathing it in, all of it in, allowing the energy to set the rhythm with your breath. Feeling the energy turning up in your body, breathing the angelic energy of the chakra system, breathing it in as one.*

Breathing the colors until they blend, breathing in and out of the chakra system until you feel that it is time and then the connection of the cosmos and the connection of the earth begin to blend and you breathe it with your hands and you breathe it in and breathe it out and it widens out and it creates this huge ,as wide and big and as huge and as wide as the earth and then the hand gestures continue to go in and out facilitating the breath and the color going in and out of Mother Earth, breathing Mother Earth, breathing the light, all the light, absorbed which creates the black hole, all of the light reflected that creates the beautiful white light.

"Angel Sarah is there more that you would have me do, is there more that you would say?"

At this point the energy is really flowing and I am shaking all over. My jaw is trembling, and I am breathing rhythmically. Then the energy blended into Angel Michael, *I am Angel Michael, I am the Angel of the breath. I am the Angel of the breath. I am that angelic point where the breath breathes into that point of blackness where it is all absorbed into one, which creates that black center of Mother Earth. This is a human understanding, I am Angel Michael, step back dear one. We are Archangel Michael, we are the Angel that cares for your safety on this planet and throughout all dimensions and all timelines. We are the Angel of space. We have been showing you the black and your humanness makes you hesitate because of preconceived ideas, but we are showing you the space, the black where all is absorbed, where all information and knowings come from.*

You ask what our role is. We are the doorway, we are the point between one dimension and the next. We represent the doorway; the access. The access between timelines and dimensions. You are struggling with this, but it is right that you will practice these techniques and be able to speak from experience. The access of dimensions and timelines and realms for the highest good of humanity. Through utilizing the chakra system, the human can step between these worlds. It does require practice dear one, utilizing the frequencies of the colors. We are showing you the white, these are human words Kelly, but for the sake of discussion let us use them. The point of the white light above the chakra system is the opening to that end of the continuum of the frequencies. The point of Angel Michael is the point of the absorption of all, and the white is the reflection of all.

"Can you explain that better?"

When you breathe the colors altogether and you run the frequency, as we have been training you to do, you run the light and the energy through this system and it is all of it Kelly. It is a very complex thing for you to understand. But it is the connection to the ability for the balancing and depositing and the picking up and the alchemizing that happens on the cosmic end or the white end for the human understanding. And the earth side or the vastness, the blackness, the space, however you would want to say it, the infinity side which is the other side. It is all beautiful and it is all one. It is all part of the whole you have to have the all to be balanced, to be that point in the middle, dear one. The utilization of the chakra system as a whole, going from understanding of each individual piece, but then realizing it's one living, breathing, unit of energy, that is here to facilitate the human experience. Breathing in and out in all directions, as we have shown you in your mind, that beautiful bursting that came from Mother Earth out to the cosmos and back again. That is the purification, that is the healing, that is the gift that all humans are striving for. Working with and spending time in that space, using the power of the breath, as we did in the middle of this (download),*and you felt the altercation begin and the tingling throughout your body, let us do that again. We will speak it through for your understanding…*

Narration-as the above came through they began to take me through the following process. They moved my hands and positioned my body. Then they took me through the meditation, the following describes it, step by step.

You sat in meditation with your feet on the floor with your hands in a triangle at your heart thumbs together, pointer fingers together, and you begin to breathe gently. As you begin to feel the oneness you sensed the I Am presence within your body, you felt the I Am presence within your body. Then you breath into it, and you breathe it out, with your intention you begin to see the colors of the points along the chakra system, and you see the colored energy start to pulsate and puff with your breaths. Balancing with your intention, setting your intention to balance, with your thumbs to your third eye, taking in a breath, your hands move down, palms out at your chest, rotating your hands down to your lower abdomen, pointer fingers pointing down as you exhale. Taking a breath in rotating your hands so that your pointer fingers are pointing up and your thumbs are at your heart center moving your thumbs to your third eye as you exhale, bringing it back down to your heart, on the inhale rotating it down to your pelvis on the exhale, bringing it back up to your heart center on the inhale, then with your thumbs to your third eye on the exhale let your breath find the rhythm as you do this.

Narration-you can not do this wrong. Let the energy lead you. I have been practicing this and every time I do it is different, but every time I do it is powerful. Sometimes, just breathing with the triangle at my heart is enough to help in whatever life is throwing at me! Sometimes I breath completely with the movement, that will take practice…when you feel altered just rest your hands in your lap and ride it out.

Letting your hands move along the chakra system at the speed that they want to go. Letting them, with your intention, with the sacred triangle balancing, feeling the energy turn up as you do this. It will require practice, you will get the rhythm. You will go slow until you get the rhythm and you will feel the energy begin to grow once the chakras are balanced and where they want to be. So let us do that. With your intention you are balancing your chakras. Seeing the beam of light, creating the beam of light, all of the different colors, the green the blue the indigo and Violet radiating out towards the cosmos, the green the yellow the orange and the red, radiating down to Mother Earth

I am Archangel Michael I have always been with you. Within this earth school, keeping you safe, giving you the connection to Mother Earth. (This feels like the culmination of all of the chakras, I believe that this process has the ability to adapt itself to each individual human as they do it. I'm trying very hard to describe what they are showing me in my mind, with a knowing, and a feeling. It's breathing together, you have to start as the human, breathing your own energy, getting your energy to build, building, building out, I'm seeing something that looks like an energy tube around me ,getting bigger and bigger around me, the energy is flowing). *That is when you would be doing the hand gestures for a bit, that's what we'll balance if life has made one or the other of your chakras out of balance, then the hand gestures will go up and down and that will facilitate the balancing and the blending of all. Then as you feel, you will feel the impulse to let your hands just sit, you'll know that part of the work is done and then you will just breathe, you'll just breathe and cycle the energy until you can feel that you are breathing for Mother Earth, you are one with Mother Earth. You are breathing into the center of Mother Earth and blowing the energy out and bringing the energy in and blowing the energy out to be connected with all, all one beautiful, beautiful energy, all one. One, one, all oneness, all oneness.*

Narration-this is a gift from our angels to us. To be used by each of us in whatever way resonates. There is no right and wrong you will let the energy show you what to do. This was a very intense download. It's the first time that two angels came through at the same time I believe that it is because they are so closely linked, think about it, the point where the human energy system ends and the earth's energy system begins. That is very literal, but it is a picture that makes sense to me right now.

It is another way to turn up our light. When we are connected and with our intention, administering to the energy of the All we are a blessing to the All. We are gifting humanity and Mother Earth, with our very breath. This process ministers to the individual human but it also ministers to the All, the consciousness and creative force that is within everything on this planet, within this planet, and beyond this planet. This is a journey my friends. We are all on this journey together, and we are all on this journey as individuals. We all do the best we can at any given moment. They are reminding me as I write this that any time, we do any conscious, deliberate activity, to turn up our light, it never goes away. It is creating beautiful threads of energy that build a bridge between human consciousness to across the veil.

It takes energy and effort to coordinate your breath with the energy flow. It is much easier to just sit in the energy and breath naturally. But this is where it began for me, all those years ago, when I practiced the Wim Hoff breathing technique and it opened the door to the universe. This is the power that they are showing us. Remember it all benefits…Let your own guides lead you, if something dose not feel good, back off. This is a life long practice, there is no getting it wrong and there is no getting it done. You will likely feel very altered and "out of it" when you do this correctly. Remember that for years the indigenous people used plant medicine to meet their spirit guides. We are using our angels and the gift of our breath…

Color-red

Body parts-hips, legs, feet, bones, teeth, adrenals.

Well, that is it, much to my shock and amazement! All of the angels came through just as Angel Ariel promised me. I hope you can take from this what resonates in your heart and that it blesses your life in whatever way it is meant to. Until next time, remember they are with you always, just breathed into your heart and ask….With much love and appreciation, *Kelly*

Kelly lives on Silver Lake with her husband Mike in a small town in Maine. They enjoy spring fishing and camping in the North Maine woods. They love to snow mobile and stay away for weekends in the winter. They ride their motorcycle in the summer time, when Mike is not working. They love their pontoon boat and summer days with their children, grandchildren and pets.

Kelly is an RN and recently retired from 23 years teaching the CNA program at the local career and technical education school.

In 2022 , during her last year of teaching she began to develop her spiritual abilities. She has written one book, ReDefining Faith, available on Amazon that tells her story. She finished Establishing Your Frequency thirteen months after she channeled her guides, Lacroose for the first time.

Kelly sees clients one to one or in groups, in person or remotely. She does channeled readings, mediumship readings, and provides spiritual mentoring. You can contact her at kellybowker7@gmail.com or call her at 207-290-7796 for more information.

You can also find her on Facebook-Kelly Nute Bowker or follow her FB page-Kelly Bowker, Medium

Made in the USA
Las Vegas, NV
14 January 2024

84360684R00085